I0488761

# The "TRUTH" about "FLIPPING" FORECLOSURE REAL ESTATE

## by: David W. Bolick

43 year Broker/Owner
Network Real Estate, Inc.

Copyright © 2014 by David W. Bolick. 618128

ISBN:   Softcover        978-1-4990-0459-5
        EBook            978-1-4990-0458-8

All rights reserved. No part of this book may
be reproduced or transmitted in any form or by
any means, electronic or mechanical, including
photocopying, recording, or by any information
storage and retrieval system, without permission in
writing from the copyright owner.

Rev. date: 05/06/2014

To order additional copies of this book, contact:
Xlibris LLC
1-888-795-4274
www.Xlibris.com
Orders@Xlibris.com

# CONTENTS

# LET ME SHOW *"YOU"* HOW TO MAKE MILLIONS USING MY POWER BUY PROGRAM

*I bought this home for $2.65 and*
*SOLD it in 6 DAYS for $128,000!!*
*I'll show YOU how !!*

# NOT !!!!!!!

## LIES, LIES, LIES, LIES!

**This Book Exposes the Truth Behind the Hype and How You <u>CAN</u> Make Legitimate Money Buying, Selling or FLIPING Real Estate**

# YOU CAN MAKE BIG MONEY BUYING & RE-$ELLING REAL ESTATE FORECLOSURES

## THIS BOOK IS ABOUT THE "TRUTH". NOT ABOUT THE, PLATITUDES, PROPAGANDA, POLLYANNA, HYPE and FICTION!

Written by David W. Bolick, 43-year Licensed Real Estate Broker practitioner

*I originally sold this eBook on eBay many years ago, but after a professor from a university in Washington state had purchased it and called to ask permission to reprint and distribute to students in his real estate class, I thought I might ought to take this a little more serious, expand it and make it a bit more professional.*

=================================================================

# WARNING:
# LET ME BE PERFECTLY CLEAR !!

As you read this book . . . keep in mind . . . there are FOUR (4) INGREDIENTS that will make you a Success or a Failure in the Real Estate Foreclosure Buying and Selling business:

**#1 FINDING the Right Property**
**#2 BUYING the property at the RIGHT PRICE**
**#3 Making the CORRECT repairs**
**#4 SELLING at the CORRECT PRICE**

Missing any one of these 4 Ingredients, can make the entire difference between Success or Failure!!

=================================================================

# INTRODUCTION

First let me say I'm actually 110 years old, give or take a few years. You surely think I'm kidding or just plain whacko, but you've seen the ads on radio or TV where a law firm asserts one attorney has been licensed for 33 years, another 31 and 2 with 22 years experience and they summarize that by implying their firm has 108 YEARS of Collective experience. Well, I'm not sure how valid a representation that is of collective knowledge since it's not all in the same brain, but if it's good enough for a law firm, it's good enough for me to also use the same analogy. Therefore, taking the number of years I've worked starting at age 7 through 63, mostly working 10 to 18 hour days and mostly 7 days a week, and comparing the Benchmark of a 40 hour workweek for the Average person . . . ok . . . I'm 110 years old. So consider all that "working knowledge" in one brain rather than the combination of 4 as above. And following is my crazy Mathematical Calculation of this FACT. This is, by the way, as scientific as the Made Man Global Warming Computer projections, so let's don't poke too many holes in it.

| Workaholic Age vs Average Person Age | | | | | |
|---|---|---|---|---|---|
| **Does not take into consideration of Sick Days, Vacation Days or time Unemployed or Between Jobs | | | | | |
| | Hours Per Week | Hours Per Year | | Hours @ Age 40 | Hours @ Age 50 | Hours @ Age 60 |
| **Average Person** | | | | | | |
| Starts Working @ age 21 on average | 40 | 2,080 | | 41,600 | 62,400 | 83,200 |
| **YEARS OLD by 40 hr workweek standard | | | | 40 | 50 | 60 |
| | | | | =41600/40/52)+20 | =(62400/40/52)+20 | =(83200/40/52)+20 |
| **Workalcoholic:** | | | | | | |
| Starts @ age 7 to 16 (10) | 10 | 520 | (1) | 5,200 | 5,200 | 5,200 |
| Starts @ age 17 to 22 (6) | 60 | 3,120 | (2) | 18,720 | 18,720 | 18,720 |
| Starts @ age 23 to 60 (38) | 82 | 4,264 | (3) | 102,336 | 144,976 | 187,616 |
| TOTAL | | | | 126,256 | 168,896 | 211,536 |
| **YEARS OLD by 40 hr workweek standard | | | | 61 | 81 | 102 |
| **Plus 4 years to age 64** | | | | | | **110** |

(1) 520 hrs per yr for 10 yrs
(2) 3,120 hrs per yr for 6 yrs
(3) 4,264 hrs per yr for 24 yrs

So in regular "average Joe years", I've been in the real estate business for over 43 years with a combined one-brain experience of 110 years.

I got in to the Real Estate business by accident in 1969. I was getting married at 19 and you have to be 21 to own real estate so I petitioned the court to have my minority disability removed to become a legal adult and bought a house at 19 years old. I bought 1514 Florida Street in Little Rock for $6,500. A 2 bedroom 1 Bath home with 838 square feet, which at today's value puts this house at $80,000.

After living in the house for 2 years and working in the printing business, a Realtor put a card on my door saying "If you want to sell your home, I have a buyer for $14,000. Now being a entrepreneur, my eyes got wide and saw a $7,000, 100% profit. So I contacted a real estate appraiser and they told me my house was worth about $9,500. Well to say the least that rather ticked me off. So I had my printing coworker make an offer on my house for $14,000 and he was approved for a bank loan and the appraiser appraised the house at a miraculous $14,000. I paid the $200 closing cost and 30 days later he deeded the house back to me by Quitclaim deed and I made the payments on the loan from there on and assumed his loan a year later.

At this point I'm thinking . . . wow . . . this "Real Estate" stuff is a money making venture and I've got to get in this business!! So I obtained my Broker's license at age 21. Then I learned that my first "transaction" wasn't such a at-arms-length transaction as they say. I had a full time job at night in the printing business and worked for a Real Estate Company during the day.

So during my Real Estate work history, I sold real estate a little over a year before going to work for a apartment management company. During that 8 year tenure, I sold and managed residential and commercial property in several states as well as managed over 6,000 units of multifamily housing, 8 office buildings, 2 strip centers, 4 mobile home parks, 1 restaurant and 4 hotels. My experiences started early in my career working with one of the premier Tax Shelter Syndication firms back in the 80's when tax sheltered real estate investments were the cutting edge investment for the wealthy. That firm eventually was forced into bankruptcy after the IRS, with a mission to close down Tax Shelter firms making widespread use of the "Rule of 78's" tax accounting. During my 8 years there, I served as a corporate officer of several corporations and real estate Property Manager as well as a Partnership Asset Manager. As things evolved, I became the point person for the Bankruptcy Trustee in the liquidation of all real estate and financial assets. You might say my 8 years experience taught me more about what "<u>NOT</u>" to do, than what "<u>TO</u>" do. After all, there's no college course called "What Not To Do in Business". During all these years in managing and selling real estate assets, I also oversaw and implemented approximately 30 million dollars of remodeling, rehabilitation and construction.

After that endeavor, I formed my own multi-state multifamily housing management company working primarily for a multi billion dollar institutional owner for the following 18 years, managing apartment complexes. There is a sacred admonition or philosophy in running a business: "Don't put all your eggs in one basket, and IF you do, WATCH the basket closely". Well, I did the latter, but didn't keep a close enough eye on the basket. As all good things must come to an end, the owner decided to sell all the assets I managed after 18 years and I went out of business in about 24 hours. So with much thought I decided to get back into residential sales which was always a fun experience. In the Residential sales business I put my remodeling and rehabilitation knowledge to use working with many investor clients in buying, reselling and flipping real estate. You've heard the "Profit is in the Purchase". That's very true in that you cannot pay too much and then spend too much "fixing" up and then expect to get out with a profit.

I've always been one of those that like to work smarter rather than harder and when I started my current company, Network Real Estate, Inc. about 18 years ago I was looking for some niche markets in real estate that were not being served or served very well. After successfully working several new concepts I read an ad in the local newspaper about making large profits Buying Foreclosures. The ad was for a Free Seminar to tell you how to make big money in the foreclosure arena. I attended the seminar, just to find out, that they are just like all the others, not telling you much of anything Except, you need to pay them $2,500 for their 3 week school to show you how to get rich buying and selling foreclosures and they'll even back you financially as a partner!! Yeah right. I thought to myself . . . having been in the fast lane of all phases of this business and liquidating over $150 million in real estate, and all kinds of real estate at that, for over 30 years, what could they possibly teach me in 3 weeks that I don't already know or couldn't find out easy enough. As with all these type organizations I'd learned from the past, you pay the big fee, buy the books, CD's, etc and then go BUY property. Nothing I didn't already know. But I started researching and fine tuning this niche market and discovered the following information and started doing my own REAL and HONEST foreclosure work for myself and investor clients. And following is the jumpstart information without all the hype and Pollyanna . . . just the plain hard facts and truth. It's not easy . . . but it can be done with some determination and a little luck.

# LESSON #1

## HOW ARE YOU GOING TO DECIFER WHAT'S IMPORTANT?

As with any seminar, book or eBook, the biggest problem that one has in listening to a speaker or reading a book is how to extract the <u>important</u> information and the action portions in an effective way, other than yellow-highlighting lines, memorizing or writing everything said on a notepad. And in doing so, you are making assumptions that these are the most important aspects. At the end of this eBook, I have done that chore for you and summarized all the important key steps to jog your memory and that which to take action on. It would be difficult at best to just jump straight to that section, print it and start without first reading the body of the text, but after reading the text, you can then jump right straight to this Action Summary at any time and have a clear and concise list of steps and procedures to get you on your way to successful Finding, Buying, Fixing and Selling foreclosures and distressed property.

# LESSON #2

## WHAT IS A FORECLOSURE?

First of all, there is some mass distortion out there on just what a foreclosure is. You hear these ads on TV about buying and selling foreclosed property and see these big ads in newspapers and magazines and even on the internet. They want to Sell You the "List" . . . that "Magic List" of the foreclosures in your area or even better the "Pre-Foreclosures". Those are the hidden ones that no body knows about yet. They get you believing that a $250,000 house is going to get bought by an average Joe for only $100,000 with NO MONEY DOWN and at closing their going to walk out the door with a check for $10,000 in their pocket and then sell the property for $300,000 after cutting the grass and doing some touch up paint over the weekend and pocket $200,000 in profit in 45 days. Yeah right . . . if it was that easy, why would they spend all their time trying to sell YOU the method . . . why not just DO IT! Think about that.

It's because that doesn't happen. That's right . . . they're outright lies! First we need to define what a real foreclosure is. HUD, the Federal Dept of Housing and Urban Development is in the business of insuring home loans. In exchange for a lender making a loan with less down payment and making it more affordable, they guarantee the bank a certain minimum loss if the loan goes bad. So if someone buys a house with almost nothing down and doesn't make the payments, then the bank files a Foreclosure Action against the homeowner. Once foreclosed, the bank gets their money in essence back from HUD and HUD becomes the actual title holder/owner of the home. NOW it's called a HUD Foreclosure. The first thing HUD does is place this asset as they call it, with a "Asset Manager" that solely handles HUD Dispositions. This "Asset Manager" . . . another unnecessary bureaucratic layer, then selects a licensed Real Estate Brokerage Firm in the area. He puts the HUD notice in the window, hires someone to board it up and winterizes it if necessary and then obtains an appraisal. Now there's the key word . . . Appraisal. Did you catch that word? Now HUD has this agent list this house in the MLS system for the appraised value (or slightly less depending on motivation) and HUD may or may not insure the loan again, depending on whether extensive repairs need to be made. In other words, if it's a Total Piece of Crap . . . HUD won't even make a loan on it. So where ya gonna get the money? Well, there's the Conventional Loan which will be based on your superior credit rating or you can simply just pay ALL CASH, as in a Cashier's Check.

Bottom line is . . . WHERE IS THE DEAL TO BE MADE HERE? If HUD is listing this house for the appraised value, where is there a discount between buying and reselling?

In most cases there is none!!! You might in fact be buying a foreclosure but it's a house . . . just a plain ordinary house. No deals, no profits, no get rich schemes here. What you're buying is a house that "Needs Repairs". So if Tom Smith's dad passes away and his dad lived in a little house for 65 years and never made any repairs, you can pretty much figure that this is a home in very bad need of just about everything. That's called a Bargain, because it is Less Than the cost of the home next door and the one across the street, However, those homes are in excellent condition, so naturally they will sell for more. If you buy Tom's dad's house, you'll have to spend a pile of money to get it into "average" condition and THEN if you sell it, you have to sell it for more than (1) the Purchase Price of the home plus (2) the cost of the Repairs.

The same goes for the VA (Veterans Administration) and their foreclosures. And the same thing for a bank that forecloses and sells directly in the market. Banks do that when there is a Conventional Loan with no VA or FHA backing involved. An appraisal is made and it's listed for the current market value. Now there are some special situations where HUD decides they have too many properties in inventory and will "dump" the price, but you have to pay attention and watch for this to happen. HUD is also more reasonable in the "appraisal" value than a typical homeowner. Take for example a average home owner in comparison. They own the home; live it in; love it; and think everyone else should too. They also think an appraisal is just one persons opinion and that THEIR house is worth a LOT more. And if someone wants their house bad enough, they will pay well above the appraised value. Folks . . . that DOES NOT HAPPEN. HUD, on the other hand, knows their house is "below the average market" because it needs repairs and all buyers want and expect "some discount" for buying a home that has to be fixed up. So even though they start with an appraisal, they may very well list it for sale somewhere below that amount for a quicker sale.

The other factor with HUD foreclosures is, they can ONLY be purchased by a "owner occupant" for the first week listed, which means they are NOT available to an "investor" . . . like YOU! So if it is a Tremendous Bargain . . . you may never even have a shot at it. If the home doesn't sell in the first week then it goes up for bid to "all bidders" UNLESS HUD decides they will "extend" the Owner Occupant status for another week or another.

Another factor is YOU as a buyer CANNOT purchase a HUD foreclosure on your own as you could with a direct homeowner. You MUST have a Real Estate Agent involved. And not all real estate agents can sell a HUD home. The real estate company has to "register" annually to be eligible to sell a HUD home and the process is done totally on-line with strict procedures.

So, to this point, you can see that Bargain Foreclosures are not just all they appear and you most likely just can't go out and (1) find them or (2) Buy them without the assistance of a Real Estate Agent that is going to be putting some money in THEIR pockets, netting the bank or HUD even less money.

Now, back to the Bank Foreclosures. These are those homes with Conventional loans that went bad and the bank had to foreclose. So what happens to those? Well, first of all, the bank files the foreclosure action for non payment and unless the homeowner is brain damaged they do one of several things . . . they either make a renewed agreement with the bank . . . a workout to get current OR they file bankruptcy to protect their assets and give them time to sell the house OR they just up and sell the house before the bank foreclosure is finalized. Not to mention that the process from start to finish for a bank foreclosure could be as much as a YEAR before the bank obtains the legal right to sell. So a very high percentage of those troubled loans never become a foreclosure or available for purchase. So when you subscribe to one of those time-wasting "Foreclosure List" which has all these "secret Pre-Foreclosures" . . . . that's what we're talking about and you'll find after spending tons and tons of hours that 90% of those homes drop off the radar screen. They were "worked out" and you never had a chance.

I worked the Pre-Foreclosure angle for a couple of years. And what I did was pick the right house in the right area that looked fairly decent and then did all of my due diligence research on the home as to Current Value and the Potential Sales Value and even pulled county records to see the amount of the mortgage and calculated the amount the owner probably had outstanding. If for example, I determined that the owner had a loan balance of approximately $100,000 and the home could sell for $120,000 or more, then that could be a potential candidate. However, if that Market Value appeared to be at or below the $100K, then it's a lost cause speaking with the owner because there is NO EQUITY.

But on those that did seem to have potential, having my ducks in a row, I knocked on the door. Now I can tell you right now . . . when someone knows they are facing foreclosure, they DO NOT answer the door for anybody. So I left a "note" on their door, that I previous had hand written that said "I am a real estate broker working with Investors that help home owners facing foreclosure where they might purchase your home and save your credit". Or something to that effect. Well, you can figure that about 1 in 10 will call me. And you can figure that 9 in 10 of those people that called are thinking that I'm an "Angel" sent down from Heaven, specifically to Save Them. And my job is to Pay Off their mortgage because they are nice people. And then my "Investor" becomes a Private Bank!! And then they will make the payments to him. OR this "Savior" investor is wanting to "loan them" the money to catch up on all their back payments with, "cross my heart promise" to pay it back later. Now, don't ask me why, they jump to this conclusion but believe me, that's what happens.

So in 2 years of working this angle and putting some 75 to 100 notes on doors, I was able to get ONE person to invite me in his home to find out just what I had to offer. Once he found out that I was not an Angel, but rather my investor was willing to give him $500 or $1,000 cash for moving money, in exchange for selling his property to my investor for the amount of all his loans, his hopes were lost. In this one particular case though, the man had 3 mortgages so we eventually wound up buying it on the court house steps. I tell the story in detail later. It turned out to be a very good FLIP house but it was a RARE situation where there were multiple mortgages that are NOT the same mortgagee which enabled this to happen. Otherwise the bank would have purchased this home for $120,000, being the total of all three of their mortgages and there would not have been a "bargain".

Those that do get foreclosed on have a logical reason. THINK ABOUT THAT STATEMENT. The house has deteriorated so much that the amount of the loan is higher than the value of the house . . . the owner got one of those 110% loan deals with a 2nd mortgage and sometimes even a 3rd mortgage which all added up, again exceed the market value of the house and there just plain isn't any equity in the house. So where's the bargain here? Again . . . None. If the value of the home is $150,000 and the loan is for $160,000, the bank would love to find someone willing to buy it for the loan balance. So on these houses, they must go though the legal foreclosure process. When the first mortgage holder (bank) proceeds with the foreclosure, this process will generally erase all liens and debts against the house that have been "noticed up" as they say, meaning that a title search has been done to determine anyone and everyone having a claim "on record" against that house . . . they are notified of the foreclosure in writing, and when the gavel goes down at the courthouse steps, and the house sells for only the amount of the first mortgage balance, everyone else, if any, gets zero and can never collect a dime on the lien they had which might be a unpaid Roof repair lien, a 2nd or even 3rd mortgage. Exceptions are priority liens like having the IRS involved, but that's usually pretty rare. If the 2$^{nd}$ and 3$^{rd}$ mortgage are also with the same lender, then the lender's bid is the total of all mortgages. If that were the case, the Loan Officer that made those loans is probably working at Burger King today. These are the procedures for the sales called "Court House Steps" which are literally sold in the county court house.

About 2009 or thereabouts, it started becoming popular for a bank to hedge their inevitable loss from a foreclosure and work with the owner and allow the owner to (1) stay in the house (2) place it for sale with a Realtor (3) and sell for less than the amount of the actual mortgage. That's called a Short Sale. Short . . . . of the Mortgage amount. There's a whole host of problems with short sales. Short sale rules vary from one lender to another, but in my experience, they have been known to come off the amount of the mortgage by as much as 25%. But, the question here is, if you're buying a house 25% below the amount of the mortgage, does that mean it is "below" the market value for similar homes in the area? In most cases no. But any conventionally financed home facing a foreclosure action, has the potential to be bought as a short sale purchase but those homes already listed with a real estate company are usually not candidates. What I'm referring to here, as far as a bargain, are homes for sale which the agent states they must SELL QUICK to beat a foreclosure. Nine out of ten times, I tell my buyer, let's just wait until it's foreclosed and deal with the bank on a price that's probably much less than what their asking now. Keep in mind that the "amount" of the sale is again based on the Current Appraised Value even though it's less than what the mortgage is. I say "Appraised Value" but most banks now-a-days have so many foreclosures, to reduce the cost of valuations in paying an appraiser $450, they first attempt to hire Realtors to perform what is called a BPO "Broker Price Opinion". There's a LOT of DANGER for a real estate agent performing BPO's for a $25 to $100 "fee", far less than what an appraisal cost because it is NOT an "Appraisal" and if they imply that, they could lose their real estate license. So basically a BPO is a Realtor looking at a home and coming up with a "fair market comparison" of what the house should sell for. However, 90% of the time or better, the agent DOES NOT even go inside the house . . . it's called a Drive By Assessment. So be on guard.

When I say Danger for an agent, what I am referring to is the Real Estate Broker that is personally in charge and responsible for all the acts of every agent in their company. There are laws specific to Real Estate Agents governed by a Real Estate Commission. And those Commission's are very protective of the Appraisers that make "Appraisal Valuations". Real Estate Agents are NOT allowed to make "Appraisals" even though the term is sometimes loosely used. That's why it's called a BPO. A Broker as well as the agent could lose their license if they used the term Appraisal. But the Bank's don't need an official "appraisal", but rather a good idea of what the property would sell for IF they had to foreclose, so it's a lot less expensive for them to pay an agent anywhere from $25 to $100 for their "Opinion" of sales amount.

So you're getting the drift here that our potential list of Huge Profit Foreclosures is dwindling fast. HUD foreclosures are generally out, as well as VA foreclosures. The conventional loans look like dead deals because there's no equity to begin with and the "preforeclosures" are a waste of valuable time, since odds are they will get worked out with the owner, coupled with the fact they are in a state of denial and won't talk to you to begin with. So what's left? Surely there is something out there to tout as Big Money in the foreclosure business. Well there is, but it's not as EASY TO FIND as they lead you to believe.

### KEY WORDS AT THIS POINT . . ."NOT EASY TO FIND"

I will say, of all these situations above, the HUD foreclosures are generally the best situations to watch for using the HUD real estate site direct, found at the HUD Home Store web address, http://www.hudhomestore.com/Home/Index.aspx The reason I say this is because (1) there are times mistakes are made as to the actual size of the house or (2) the appraised value is way underestimated. I've seen a 3 bedroom 2 bath home with 2,000 square feet listed as a 2 bedroom 1 bath home with 1,100 square feet . . . you have to pay attention and go look at each home with a Drive By and do your own research. Also, HUD doesn't like a house on the market too long. If it doesn't sell in a short period of time, they are the first to accept a very low offer or lower the price. If you look at the "History" section in a MLS Listing, you might notice that like every 2 months they drop the price by $10,000 so if you're close to that next drop date, either make the offer lower or wait. But even though these great HUD foreclosures can be a good deal, and many times a _very_ good bargain . . . it's still NOT a $20,000 house worth $200,000 like you see on these hyped up TV ads. You'll be doing a excellent job if you get it 25% below the market and 40% below the "potential" market after some work. Investors generally won't buy without at least 25% below Market Value.

A note on the Short Sale properties. The Banks don't play fair many times. The bank allegedly agrees to take less than the mortgage amount but they don't necessarily put the exact amount "in writing" and it's always subject to some Committee approving the sale, along with the home owner. So they might say they will take $75,000 when the mortgage is $90,000 but it might take them 6 months to approve the sale, if they do, or they might just up and change their mind completely. Generally if you're buying a house to live in, Short Sales are too much of a headache to even chase after, but if you're chasing it as an investment to rent or flip, time is not that much of a factor. You don't have to worry with a Title Binder like a Courthouse Foreclosure on these properties though, especially if there is a Realtor involved.

# LESSON #3

## WHERE ARE THE "REAL" FORECLOSURES?

Let me begin this by sighting some real examples I've been involved in and you can see where the real foreclosures and distressed special situations are that you can find. Later I identify some other investment opportunities that are just as good if not better than the popular "foreclosure" property. These are a few of my actual cases.

### #1-LEAWOOD ADDITION—$70,000 PROFIT—40 DAYS:

There was a home in a nice stable upper middle class neighborhood that showed up on the Court House Steps foreclosure list, which by the way is published in many places and we'll cover that later. I pulled the tax record using the "free" online county service and saw where the house was valued by the county at about $180,000. It also stated the house had about 2,400 square feet and was a 3 bedroom 2 bath. The legal notice stated the mortgage being foreclosed on was dated less than 2 years ago. That would indicate that there is probably no equity. The notices don't reveal the amount of the mortgage. I went to the county clerk's office and had them pull the deed record, which by the way is now On-Line, and it showed a mortgage in the amount of $90,000 was taken out about 2 years ago. That appeared strange because the ownership hadn't changed. One could conclude that the owner was just borrowing some money for whatever reason and using their home as collateral for that loan. I tried to personally talk to the owner on the phone and discovered that there was a 40+ year old unemployed daughter living there with her mother who was the owner of the house. As the story eventually unfolded, the daughter got ill, moved in with mom . . . took mom's house that had no mortgage . . . got a loan for $90,000 . . . Apparently blew the money in about a year and then stopped making payments on the loan. So the bank was filing a foreclosure. Now had the owner cooperated with me, I could have told them they had many options. Sell the house and pay off the loan and have a good sum to live on . . . file a bankruptcy and protect their asset until they could do a workout with the bank, etc. But instead the daughter was, how shall we say, a bit short in the brains department and she was in a state of denial. She also had apparently been lying to mom about what was going on.

Bottom line was the foreclosure came up at the court house steps and on that particular day only a handful of foreclosure investor buyers were in attendance. So my partner and I bought the house for $97,000 with a starting bid of about $90,000. Now we owned a $180,000 house for $97,000, which by the way . . . you have to pay for it in "all cash" within 24 hours . . . something the foreclosure pump artists fail to mention. Next it was my job to evict mom and daughter and get possession of the house, which took about 30 days and then we spent about $10,000 doing some fixing and painting and sold the house in about 40 days for $188,000. So the net profit was about $70,000 after all expenses and my partner and I split the money. That's the story-book, dream-come-true, that's-how-easy-it-is example that all the hype and books and schools thrive on telling you about. Granted, it was real and it really happened, but the question is . . . just how often does that happen? Just how easy is it to find such a special situation deal? We worked together for the next 5 years and never came across another deal that good or that easy.

## #2-CEDAR RIDGE ADDITION—$20,000 PROFIT—45 DAYS

Ok, here was our second deal, as mentioned previously about the 3 mortgages. The house originally popped up on the foreclosure notices and my research showed it to be a house that should sell for about $125,000. The 1st mortgagee was foreclosing and research showed after visiting with this nice gentlemen for about an hour, that he in fact actually had THREE separate mortgages. The good news from an investors standpoint is that all 3 mortgagees were different. In other words the first mortgage was with ABC Bank and the 2nd mortgage was with DEF Bank and the 3rd was GHI Bank. What that means is that after the 1st mortgagee forecloses, the other 2 mortgages will be completely erased. The deal is that a 2nd mortgagee NEVER bids for their own mortgage because they would have to also purchase the 1st mortgage and be in more debt than where they started. So all they can do is pray that the 1st is low enough that investors will bid up the price enough for them to get whole or at least some money. Now this was not a bad deal at all, because the first mortgage wasn't but about $75,000. Now the owner can't sell because his total mortgages added up to about $126,000 and the maximum value of the home was about $125,000, not to mention the costs involved in selling. Now if the foreclosure bidding ended at $80,000 then the 1st mortgagee would get 100% of what they're owed and the 2nd mortgagee would get $5,000 with the 3rd getting none.

So, again my partner and I bided on the court house steps and got this house for $95,000. So the 1st mortgagee got all their money and the 2nd mortgagee got about $20,000 which was almost all they were owed. By the time we paid All Cash for it within 24 hours, the owner had already moved out. We spent about $5,000 in fix up and sold the house within 30 days for $123,000 and profited about $20,000 in 45 days. Again, not bad. But the unique special situation here was that the 3 mortgagees were all different banks. Most of the time, there are only 2 mortgages at best, and they are all with the same bank, which means the bank would have bided over $95,000 and the bank would have bought the house because we wouldn't have bided any higher.

## #3-SPRING VALLEY LAKE—PROJECTED PROFIT $130,000—3 MONTHS. ACTUAL OUTCOME $15,000 PROFIT—6 MONTHS

Another great house popped up on the foreclosure radar screen and my partner and I both knew this one would have a LOT of bidders, which would drive the price up too high, so I put on my investigator hat and started trying to locate the owner of this vacant house with 220 feet of frontage on a lake. With regard to this house, let me say here that I put on my (CSI) <u>Comprehensive Search Investigator</u> hat in finding out information. More on that later. I found a name and I found an address on the tax bill that was different than the address of the house. Now what that generally means is that the owner of the house doesn't live there and has the tax bill mailed to the address of the home he does live in. So then I did a reverse address search on-line (more info on that later as well) and called the name of the person that lived at that location. I started by saying "hello, my name is David Bolick in Little Rock, is this Mr. John Smith? And he says No. So I say "I'm trying to find Mr. John Smith that owns a house at 123 Easy Street here in Little Rock, that is being foreclosed on and I have someone that will pay cash for it and SAVE his credit". At first he was reluctant to tell me anything, but said he knew the guy I was looking for and would have him call me. The foreclosure was to take place on the following Tuesday and this was a Wednesday. The guy called within a matter of minutes, and we worked out a verbal deal to buy his house for the amount of his first mortgage and all selling costs which came to about $110,000. We made the offer direct to him via emailing the contract and him signing, scanning and emailing back, and I presented it to the foreclosure servicing company conducting the court house foreclosure that was coming up Tuesday. To say the least, they were highly pissed off that we were messing up there routine foreclosure, but they were obligated by law to contact their client, the mortgagee, and tell them there was an all cash offer ready to close in less than 24-hours prior to the courthouse sell. So they approved the sale and we saved the guy a foreclosure on his record and got a great house. Or so we thought.

I mean, you tell me. Seriously. A 3,000 square foot 2 story house with a split level floor plan with 220 feet of footage on a large lake with big huge glass windows all across the back of the home overlooking the lake with a 100 yard winding private driveway to the home deep in a wooded area with 4 bedrooms 3 1/2 baths, 2 fireplaces, one up and one down, huge den, 2 car garage, double decks off the back of the house sitting on about an acre of land right in the middle of the city that most people don't even know the area where 300 homes exists. The county showed a Value of $240,000 and physically it just looked like it needed a lot of cosmetic work and with some enhancements it could be a HOME RUN!

Here is where I was reminded of a large commercial apartment complex I was selling years prior, and the astute commercial salesman asked me "David, what Unexpected things do you Expect to go wrong in the next few years"? Say What?

Our plan was to spend about $20,000 which is much more than average, to repaint the entire exterior and interior, repave the 12' wide asphalt driveway, add a 30' by 30' deck off the master bedroom overlooking the lake, install ceramic tile on the bathroom floors and turn the half bath downstairs into an easy large full bath and remove some small standard windows downstairs and install some large 4′ x 5′ glass windows overlooking the lake. Then sell for $260,000+.

Somewhere between "finding" this house and "buying it", my Investor Partner had a dream that I agreed to be "on the property every day, 8 hours a day, supervising all our Rescue Mission day-labor workers" until we were ready to put it on the market. But seeing the profit here I went ahead.

So about 2 weeks in to the job, we had about 8 house leveler experts leveling the house and wanted to remove an old custom bar built in the center inside wall facing the lake downstairs den. I'm standing about 8 feet from the outside of the house on the back lakeside when they busted out the bar and all of a sudden HOUSTON . . . WE HAVE A PROBLEM! Little did we know, ALL of the downstairs interior walls were completed rotted and only being held up by this little 5′ x 7′ bar in the center of the den. Once that was knocked out, the entire house literally BROKE IN HALF and I thought the whole thing was going to fall on me. Luckily with that crew there, they took about 10 power jacks, lifted the top of the house back up, took about 15 six by six post and re-secured the structure before I got killed. To say the least, this shot the cost of repair Out The Roof !!!

In the end, after 6 months of hard work, we finished and got an appraisal of $235,000. We were NOT happy. I told the appraiser and she went back in and did some surgery and came up with an appraisal of $260,000. This deal should have produced a major windfall profit, BUT, the repair fixup jumped to $85,000 AND our regular contractor decided he didn't want to do the job and we only made about $15,000 on the deal after a bunch of hard and agonizing work. We were lucky to keep from going in the hole. So as you can see, this is a 3rd method of buying a foreclosure or Pre-Foreclosure or a Distressed piece of property . . . direct from the owner being foreclosed on, that has nothing to lose either way, but can at least salvage his credit record. The key here is "finding" the missing person. And by all rights this should have been a $130,000 profit in 3 months, but you just can't be too careful. You can do all the due diligence in the world, but seeing through walls is not something on that list. So, always Expect the Unexpected, like that commercial salesman asked me years ago.

## #4-NOB HILL ADDITION—$70,000 EQUITY AT PURCHASE

The next two such deals I did in the last six months were owner occupants wanting "Investor" bargains. First was a investor that called me about a HUD foreclosure that was Owner Occupant Only at the time and she wanted to see it in case it turned "All Bidder". I pulled all the information including tax records, mortgage history, comps, MLS Listing, HUD listing, HUD Physical Condition Report and we looked at the house with our flashlights, since all HUD homes have no utilities. I noticed that the listing showed it was a 2 bedroom 1 bath with 1,100 square feet and the MLS Listing also showed that, however the house was actually a 3 bedroom 2 bath house with 2,000 square feet. The inside was Immaculate!!! I mean almost in perfect condition, excellent carpet, painting, new kitchen cabinets, appliances, etc. This was an obvious Rehab job. There was nothing wrong with this house. My investor was stunned and wanted to know why in the world this house hasn't sold. I told her probably because 90% of buyers are looking for 3 bedroom homes and this shows 2 bedroom so it's just not pulling up on the radar.

Now keep in mind this house has a partially under ground downstairs and has been shut up with no air movement for several months and it did smell rather "musky" inside. Quite common. My buyer still thought it had something to do with "mold"... that someone probably attempted to buy it and backed out because of deadly mold. I assured her that any home that is shut up will get some mildew inside and that isn't a problem. The VALUE of this house looked to me to be about $175,000 with a few minor upgrades and HUD was asking $98,000. So she made an offer and it was accepted. Then she backed out of the deal because despite having obtained an Environmental Mold Report clearing the house, she still felt uncomfortable. So a woman calls me up out of the blue to see a foreclosure in a similar quality neighborhood and the house was an absolute disaster! They were asking about $115,000 in a $150,000 neighborhood but I wouldn't have personally given you $10,000 for this house. It had major roof leaks, all the wood was rotted on the floors, there was Black Mold a half inch thick on the walls downstairs to the point I was actually afraid to be breathing the air. I asked her what kind of house she was looking for and she basically described this 3 Bedroom HUD foreclosure my investor just backed out of, so we headed over there and the next thing you know, my new client, a investor Owner-Occupant, bought this HUD house for around $90,000 that's worth at least $160,000, as is, all because in my opinion, it was improperly listed.

So DON'T take the word of a Listing Sheet that a home is exactly as they represent. Drive by.

## #5-GEYERS SPRINGS ADDITION—$40,000 EQUITY AT PURCHASE

The second investor Owner-Occupant buyer example a few months ago was regular 3 bedroom 2 bath home for sale in a middle range neighborhood that should be selling for around $60K to $80K that they were only asking $40,000. My Owner-Investor-Occupant Buyer, looking for a bargain, to buy, fix, live and sell at a later date found the house just driving around. I got him the info and we went over and looked. The house was in a curve and had over 1 acre of land where everyone else had about one-quarter acre. The inside of the house was structurally in perfect condition. You could tell it had been very well taken care of. The roof looked new and you could tell that this was probably a little old lady that had money that always had been taken to the cleaners by repair people doing overkill on doing more work than necessary. I told my buyer this house is worth at LEAST $75,000 as is. He being a Donald Trump in the making said lets make an offer of $35,000. I cautioned him... it's only been on the market for 5 days and it will sell FAST... I wouldn't play around with the house price... it's way under priced at $40,000 and I wouldn't risk losing out by low-balling them. He insisted. I wrote the offer for $35,000 and it was accepted within a matter of hours. As it turned out, the owner was 95 years old, in a nursing home and her daughter in Flordia was handling mom's business and wanted the money fast for her nursing home care. So here is a Non-Foreclosure, Non-HUD, Non-Distressed home that is just as much a bargain as any foreclosure. It had a built in $40,000 equity. This would have made a perfect, fast FLIP if that were my buyers intent.

## #6-CANDLEWOOD ADDITION—$200,000 PROFIT—9 DAYS

One of my investor friends that comes in contact with a lot of people in the public found out a customer won a large multimillion lottery in Texas. He asked him what his plans were and he said he planned to move to Texas and then travel the world. So my friend asked him what he was going to do with his beautiful 5,300 square foot, 5 bedroom, 4 1/2 bath, home with a guest house, swimming pool, 3 car garage, overlooking the river. Knowing he didn't need the money and liked my friend, he told him he could have it for $150,000. So he bought it, spent about $20,000 dressing it up later, and then I sold it for him for a LOW quick sale of $380,000 after being on the market for only 9 days. Nice $200,000 profit. All because my investor always has his eyes open, ears open and always looking for another "deal" in the making.

## #7-KANIS ROAD—$183,000 PROFIT—12 MONTHS

This is a situation where I sold my investor a sleeper HUD foreclosure consisting of 3 bedrooms, 3 baths, 2,682 square feet with a Guest House and in-ground swimming pool located in a secluded area in the middle of town on 2 acres for $97,000. This was a run down $250,000 house. Granted from a physical standpoint the 2 story contemporary house looked like it was falling down, but if you know construction and have experience in rehabbing, you know most everything can easily be fixed, including foundations. In this case, my investor bought the property and decided to move in. Spent about $20,000 fixing it up and as bad luck would have it, it caught on fire while he was asleep one night and he got the full insured value payoff of $300,000. The house burned to the ground so he's now contemplating selling the property as Commercial while living in the guest house.

And I could go on and on with other examples, but from these samples, you can see that bargains coming from a "Foreclosure List" is only one identifier of a potential candidate investment. In reality, when dealing with TRUE, raw courthouse foreclosures, you're talking about Courthouse Steps. The bank will wind up buying the house in more than 90% of the cases so there will only be 10% of the deals on the table and you've got a whole host of folks that are professionals down there competing against you for the same deal. The guys that own their own construction or remodeling business have the edge over the average guy, because they can perform the fix up a lot cheaper. So you have to broaden your focus on bargain property and not just focus on the "Foreclosure" type property.

# LESSON #4

## WHERE IS THIS FORECLOSURE LIST?

Most all foreclosures are published in your local newspaper, generally on a Sunday. Granted, some are difficult to sift though because of all the legal wording but after you read them awhile, you get used to picking out the area that has the addresses you're interested in. You need to pick a few areas of town that you're familiar with and stick to only the foreclosures in those areas. In my town, we have an additional publication called The Daily Record. It's a publication of all Legal Notices of all kinds that is mailed to all real estate agents and mortgage companies and anyone can subscribe to it. Realtors get it free. If you have a Realtor friend, I'm sure they wouldn't mind giving you their copy since there are plenty in their office.

KEEP IN MIND, you've MUST work with a Real Estate Agent to be successful. A Realtor can (1) Find the deals (2) Provide you a Free CMA (Comparable Market Analysis) of the home or a Subdivision (3) Negotiate a professional deal for you (4) Write the offer and make sure YOUR interest are all legally protected. (5) Provide invaluable information as to areas to avoid investing or areas to concentrate on. REMEMBER, when using a Realtor to BUY property . . . the SELLER PAYS 100% OF THE REAL ESTATE COMMISSION! It's FREE to YOU.

As for choosing a Realtor . . . let's be honest. You don't want a Highly Successful Super agent that works for the largest Realtor company in town that is a MultiBillion Dollar Producer. He/she doesn't have the time or patience to fool with you. You want a small to medium sized company and an agent in that company that is "pretty good" that's "HUNGRY" for business and one that has been in the business at least 3 years. If they've made it that long they are either "Producing" or have another source of household income. They will be the most helpful and treat you like you want. IF you don't have a good relationship with them after a few months, find another one and work with BOTH, or even more. As for the Foreclosure Notice publications, most major cities also have a similar publication as my city. Call your bank or a real estate agent and ask them about that kind of publication. Generally they're easier to read and sift through.

There are also several online internet companies that provide this information for all cities in the U.S., BUT, I've found their information to be stale, out of date and very inaccurate, not to mention they charge too much! But they are improving. It wouldn't hurt to subscribe for maybe a month and see what you think. Sometimes you can get a 1-month FREE subscription. There is one company that I won't name that is constantly in the national news like they were some sort of "National Authority" and when I hear a CNN or other cable news channel quote what "they" say about the real estate market . . . I cringe and think, LORD . . . those people don't know flip about the real estate market. They're nothing more than computer geek data and number source pirates. ALL their information originates from REALTORS.

You have three kinds of "Experts"; (1) Those that have tried and failed; (2) those who have read about it but never done it and (3) those that have Done It and Succeeded.

Make an arrangement with your newly selected real estate agent to provide you with CMA's (Comparative Market Analysis) on short notice and by email. A "Comparative Market Analysis" and what it is, is whatever that agent "thinks" it is. For example, if you ask me what the comparative value of a specific home is in my area . . . first, I know the physical boundaries of homes like the one your asking about and I know which similar neighborhoods to include or exclude. I'll also go in my MLS (Multiple Listing Service) and search criteria like "Sold", "Sold within the last 6 or 12 months", "Same number of bedrooms and baths", "a square footage range that is a few feet hundred feet above and below the one you asked about", etc. And of course I've already pulled the Tax Record on the house in question. That took me 20 seconds. The CMA took me another 5 minutes. Then I press the magic "CMA Summary" button and pow . . . there's the report. Then I copy, paste to an email and shoot it to you.

Now for my Special or Potential Clients I prepare a CUSTOMIZED CMA Analysis. This is where I narrow down those homes of similar criteria and "Export" that data from the MLS to an Excel Spreadsheet and then cut out the columns I don't want and add a few calculating columns. SEE BELOW. This type CMA provides a Non Professional buyer a better handle and overview on what values are NOW and what values COULD BE by using the Average Sale, Low Sale, Highest Sale and Median Sale and then applying the apple-to-apple comparison square footage to the Subject property. Now keep in mind that Appraisers do NOT use "Square Footage" as a method of determining the Value of a property. However, you WILL find that virtually all Real Estate Agents do. Appraisers get a little scientific on determining values and their assignment is defined as "The value at which the Average Buyer would pay, in a Reasonable amount of time".

I designed this concept and format myself and have used it for some 18+ years and it's not copyrighted, so feel free to use it yourself or give it to your new real estate agent and maybe they might like using it for all their clients as well.

**Meadowcliff Area Homes FOR SALE**
**Comparable to Subject - 4 Chestnut Ave**

| Address | Original Price | Current Price | Variance | Price Per Sq Foot | Square Feet | Bdrm | Baths | Days On Market | Subdivision | Status | Built |
|---|---|---|---|---|---|---|---|---|---|---|---|
| 11 Wanda Avenue | $64,900 | $64,900 | $0 | $49.17 | 1,320 | 3 | 2 | 131 | Dickey JO | Active | 1958 |
| 6814 Brookview Dr | $69,900 | $69,900 | $0 | $48.21 | 1,450 | 3 | 2 | 36 | Brookwood | Active | 1966 |
| 76 W Windsor Dr | $73,000 | $69,900 | ($3,100) | $49.93 | 1,400 | 3 | 2 | 63 | Brookwood | Active | 1966 |
| 26 S Meadowcliff | $69,900 | $69,900 | $0 | $65.63 | 1,065 | 3 | 1 | 141 | Meadowcliff | Active | 1955 |
| 21 Westmont | $74,500 | $74,500 | $0 | $50.68 | 1,470 | 3 | 1.5 | 182 | Meadowcliff | Active | 1955 |
| 74 S Meadowcliff | $74,900 | $74,900 | $0 | $64.02 | 1,170 | 3 | 2 | 8 | Meadowcliff | Active | 1958 |
| 17 N Meadowcliff Dr | $75,000 | $75,000 | $0 | $57.69 | 1,300 | 3 | 1.5 | 142 | Meadowcliff | Pending | 1958 |
| 18 Rosewood Dr | $75,000 | $75,000 | $0 | $58.78 | 1,276 | 3 | 1.5 | 142 | Brookwood | Active | 1969 |
| | | | | | | | | | | | |
| Average | $72,138 | $71,750 | | $55.51 | 1,306 | | | 106 | | | |
| High | $75,000 | $75,000 | | $65.63 | 1,470 | | | 182 | | | |
| Low | $64,900 | $64,900 | | $48.21 | 1,065 | | | 8 | | | |
| Median | $73,750 | $72,200 | | $54.19 | 1,310 | | | 136 | | | |

**Subject:**
**4 Chestnut Avenue** — 1,375

| | |
|---|---|
| Average | $76,330 |
| High | $90,246 |
| Low | $66,284 |
| Median | $74,506 |

In the above example I've taken the recent home sales in a neighborhood and then extracted only those that are like-kind in size, age and condition and identified the Average, High, Low and Median information. Then I identify the Subject house as to their square footage and apply those same per square foot calculations for a "Proposed" assumption that IF the subject house was comparable then this is the amount of what its average, high, low and median numbers would look like. In this example, I'm telling the Seller or the prospective buyer that On Average this home would sell for $76,330 but if it's in much better shape it might go as high as $90,246 and if it is in the worse of condition, you could expect a low sale of $66,284 but the median, removing the high and low peaks is around $74,506. Most of the time the Average and Median hit the nail on the head.

In summary though, you want an agent that uses email, that you can email him/her and say Fred/Rita, can you send me a CMA on 1234 Normal Street? And they'll take 15 minutes to search the MLS and email you a CMA that will tell you that your target house should sell for X dollars. Now you know how much the re-sell is. You might have to arrange a small fee for them to pull this info for you, but if you can swing them some real estate business as in a buyer or seller, they'll be glad to do this for you free any time. It's all about reciprocity. I've NEVER charged to do this and don't know any agents that do. If they want business, they don't mind.

Now . . . as for some INTERNET resources to get you jumpstarted. Following are websites you need to go to and BOOKMARK, with the exception of "my" local Real Estate Tax sites . . . you'll want to pull your particular county or parish website to bookmark. Your Number One step in all research, once you've identified a home of interest is PULL THE TAX RECORD. That tells you Who owns it, What the county says it's valued at, What they paid for it, What the history of sales have been, How many square feet it has and in many cases the number of bedrooms and baths and sometimes an exterior picture and a floor plan. NOTE: It also contains the House Address as well as the address to Mail The Tax Bill to. IF they are <u>not</u> the same . . . that would indicate the house is rented.

## = = = = = = = = RESEARCH SOURCES FOR FORCLOSURES = = = = = = = = AND OTHER PROPERTY FOR IMPORTANT DUE DILLIGENCE

You want to use or FIND the following similar sites for YOUR tax record information. Your county Tax Assessment, your Tax "Billings" and your Clerks Filings for Deeds, Mortgages, etc.

### Arkansas Real Estate Tax Records:
  → http://www.arcountydata.com/
### Arkansas Pulaski County Personal Property Tax Records:
  → http://public.pulaskicountytreasurer.net/
### Arkansas Pulaski County Clerk Records: (Deeds, Mortgages, Divorce, etc)
  → http://www.pulaskiclerk.com/

For example . . . . let's say you live in Pittsburg, Oklahoma. You'll want to do a Google search for "Pittsburg county Oklahoma Tax". Below is what you'll see, in the picture below. Then click on Pittsburg County Assessor website and BOOKMARK it.

### State of Oklahoma Real Estate Information: http://www.ok.gov/

Here is what the actual source website looks like. You can search by Parcel ID which you won't have, or by Street Address or Owner Name.

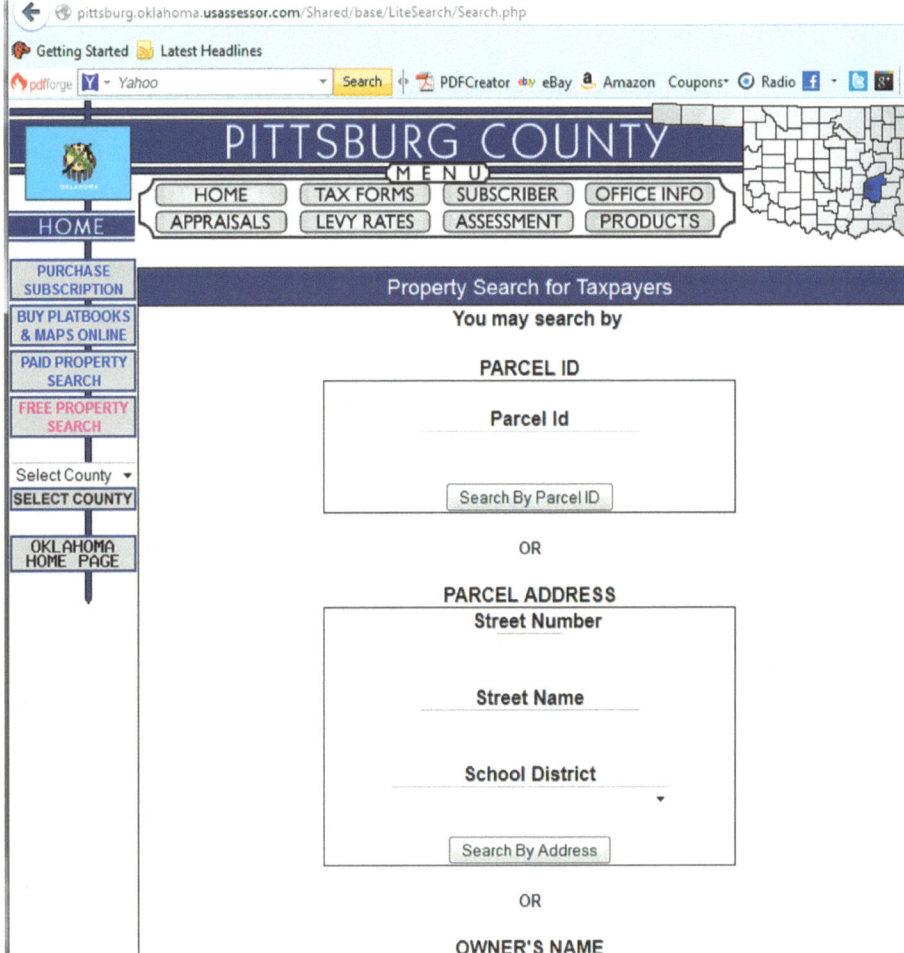

Here are your due diligence research sites on WHO we're talking about that owns this house. Use the Reverse Address or Reverse Phone search, whichever you need to find information.

### Reverse Phone, Address Lookup-National
➜ http://www.addresses.com/phone

Here we have a slue of websites with plenty of Foreclosure leads. You've got the direct HUD website, the Home Telos, Hubzu, Pemco and HomePath that all sell HUD and VA foreclosures. Then you have the FEMA maps to make sure you're not looking at a property in a flood zone. Then the VA Website, and believe it or not, you can also search the Zillow and Yahoo sites for foreclosures. The RealtyTrac site is one of the paying websites.

### HUD HomeStore foreclosures
➜ http://www.hudhomestore.com/Home/Index.aspx

**Home TelosFirst foreclosures**
→ https://www.hometelosfirst.com/Login?p_build_page=Login

**Hubzu foreclosures**
→ https://www.hubzu.com/

**PEMCO foreclosures**
→ http://hudpemco.com/

**HomePath foreclosures**
→ http://www.homepath.com/listing?listingid=41854956

**FEMA Flood Maps**
→ https://msc.fema.gov/

**VA Foreclosures:**
→ http://listings.vrmco.com/

**Zillow.com Foreclosures:**
→ http://www.zillow.com/little-rock-ar/foreclosures/

**RealtyTrac.com Foreclosures (Paid Site for Details)**
→ http://www.realtytrac.com/mapsearch/us.html

**Yahoo Foreclosures**
→ http://homes.yahoo.com/

Below you have the direct search for any home that Bank of America has foreclosed on and below that is the National Realtors Association website, Realtor.com

**Bank of America Foreclosures:**
→ http://foreclosures.bankofamerica.com/

**Realtor.com Foreclosures:**
→ http://www.realtor.com/foreclosure?source=web

Below is the Guidestar website. I think it's still free to register. If you had a need to search a nonprofit corporation, here are all their records, etc.

**NonProfit Organizations:**
→ http://www2.guidestar.org/Home.aspx

**Getting a C.L.U.E. Report** (Comprehensive Loss Underwriting Exchange)
→ http://www.lexisnexis.com/risk/solutions/clue-home-seller.aspx

If your doing some "Go it Alone" work and need some good quality Legal Forms . . . don't go to Office Depot . . . just go to this website and you can make a donation or use the form free and even edit it in Word.

**<u>Free Legal Forms:</u>**
→ http://www.ilrg.com/forms/

**<u>Some Miscellaneous Websites: (discussed later)</u>**
→ About Tax Deed Sales:
  → http://en.m.wikipedia.org/wiki/Tax_sale
→ About Tax Deed Statutes from the National Tax Lien Association
  → http://www.thentla.com/?page=Statutes
→ About Buying Tax Deed Homes from Bankrate.com
  → http://www.bankrate.com/finance/real-estate/buying-a-home-in-a-tax-lien-sale-3.aspx

# LESSON #5

## WHERE DO YOU GET THE MONEY TO BUY FORECLOSURES?

Here's the shocking news for many want-a-be foreclosure buyers. YOU CANNOT BORROW MONEY TO BUY A TRUE COURTHOUSE STEP FORECLOSURE. The nature of those foreclosure products dictate that at the courthouse steps auction that you MUST pay ALL CASH generally in less than 24 hours. There is no way possible to obtain a Real Estate Loan in less than 24 hours.

So, you either have to have credit stronger than Bears Breath, All Cash, a Line of Credit, OR a Money Investor/Partner that puts up the cash and you partner with him to split the profits. Now if you have excellent credit or financial resources, you can arrange with your bank to give you a "Line of Credit" or a preapproved "Signature Loan" so that when you are successful in a foreclosure bid, you draw on this line of credit and obtain the funds from your banker in less than 24 hours. THEN once you've paid for the house, you can then arrange for a Real Estate Loan later if you want, with your banker and regain your line of credit or cash funds. But you'll be paying double closing costs.

If you're buying any other type foreclosure type property, for example, one listed by HUD, and obtaining a Home Loan . . . remember . . . banks will loan YOU personally up to 97% of the appraised value of the home, NOT to exceed the purchase price, if you OCCUPY it, BUT, ONLY if you are an Owner Occupant. If you lie about that, it's a federal felony. So don't test the waters there. And if you are an "Investor", that is NOT going to live in the house . . . . then you are not eligible for an FHA or VA loan and must obtain a Conventional Loan and they generally want at least a 20% DOWN PAYMENT!! So that's $20,000 cash for a down payment on a $100,000 house that could be worth $185,000 . . . . so do you have $20,000 cash to put into a venture that will also need funds for Rehab? And even if you do, banks generally restrict you in the purchase of a maximum of 3 houses on that basis. So if you find 3 good deals, you're maxed out. The only place money grows on trees is the United States Federal Reserve Bank. And keep in mind that the bank will ONLY loan based on the Purchase Price OR Appraisal, WHICHEVER IS "LESS". There is no such thing as buying a home appraised for $180,000 for $140,000 and obtaining a 80% loan of $144,000 (80% of $180k) and walking out with a $4,000 check and having an instant $40,000 Equity FREE. That only happens in Dreams and Pump & Dump Illegal Scan Artists.

Now . . . there is a "potential" possibility along this line of thinking. You buy this home worth $180,000 for $140,000; you put $28,000 down (20%) and get a loan of $112,000 and then you "WAIT" for some time to pass like either after you do some remodeling or a year and THEN you go to a different lending organization and you apply for a REFINANCE of your loan. Assuming the interest rates are about the same, you now WILL get a refinance loan BASED ON THE APPRAISED VALUE AND NOT WHAT YOU PAID A YEAR AGO. So in this situation, you get a new appraisal say for $188,000 since you've made improvements and had the home for a year and the new loan will be $150,400 (80% of $188k). NOW you pay off your $140,000 loan and DO walk off with about $10,000 and still have about $38,000 in equity. This could all be done with 80% loans and you're Renting the property for the purpose of building up some Rental Income.

This will be the largest hill to climb in the whole process . . . deciding how you are going to obtain the funds to purchase. So your FIRST step before you spend a huge amount of time in searching and researching foreclosure property is TALK TO YOUR BANKER and get whatever financing arrangements made before you start, or FIND that money bags partner.

# LESSON #6

## BUYING GOVERNMENT TAX DEEDS

This is a subject I hate to even get in to. This is probably the biggest HYPE and ABUSE in advertising I've ever seen. Let me sum it up this way. If you're over 40, a multimillionaire, bored, a brilliant attorney with lots of powerful friends, then GO FOR IT. If you're not, I'd recommend you purchase a good Metal Detector and search for Meteorites in the Arizona desert and sell them on eBay . . . . you'll make better use of your time and make more money.

And the reason . . . In Arkansas, for example, you have to stop making tax payments on your real property (home) for 3 years before the county turns your deed over to the State. Then the state keeps the deed for another 2 years before they set up Tax Deed Sales in the 5th or 6th year.
The State Land Commissioner is charged with this duty for the purpose of providing a Collection Agency, for all practical purposes, by using the public as the heavy hand in getting you to pay your delinquent real estate tax OR they will sell your property to the highest bidder.

Now, in Arkansas as well as many other states, it sounds like a pretty good way to make some easy money, but there are more cautions and pitfalls than Florida has sinkholes. MOST homes have a mortgage. Secondly, MOST homes with a mortgage have a monthly payment called PITI, that being Principal, Interest, Taxes and Insurance. Lets say for example a person, for whatever reason, is on a Foreclosure selling block that owns a 3 bedroom 2 bath home valued at $125,000 with an original $120,000 mortgage loan to ABC Bank with a Total Payment (PITI) of $761.53. That being $627.26 for Principal and Interest, $90.16 per month for real estate taxes and $44.11 for home owners insurance. So the real estate taxes are $1,082 per year. Even though the owner stops making payments, this does NOT mean that ABC Bank does not pay the Real Estate Taxes, because they are Notified and they PAY those taxes and if they slip up, they will Catch Up, but they will NOT allow the Land Commissioner to take the deed to the property they have a mortgage on.

So if an owner IS on the State Land Commissioner's sell block, that means FIRST, he has NO MORTGAGE and that he currently is behind at least $5,409 in this example, not considering the penalties. So the "implication" is that you can BUY his property for the "amount of the taxes". WRONG. In Arkansas, the MINIMUM bid is the "Assessed Valuation". The County Value of this home let's say is right on the mark at $125,000. The Assessed Valuation is "20% of the Value". Most counties in most states base tax rates on Assessed Valuations which vary by percent. So if you must bid the minimum of the assessed value, that means you have to START your bid at $25,000 for a home that is behind $5,000 on its taxes.

So what if in a worse case scenario there WAS a mortgage at ABC Bank and they did NOT pay the taxes for whatever reason and you bought the Commissioners Deed for $25,000. Now . . . do you SERIOUSLY believe that YOU can buy a $125,000 house for $25,000 and NOT have to pay the mortgage to ABC Bank? NO. You didn't receive a Warranty Deed from the Land Commissioner . . . you got in essence a Quitclaim Deed meaning that whatever rights they had you now have, but it doesn't erase the mortgage.

Now in a case where the bank loan is below the required threshold of LTV, Loan to Value, meaning that an owner only owes the bank 80% or less of the value, they can pay their real estate taxes "directly" to the county rather than be required to have a monthly "Escrow" payment to the bank. In that case, the bank "might not know" that the owner hasn't paid the Real Estate Taxes. So when the Land Commissioner takes the Deed from the homeowner with the intent to sell the property by Commissioner Deed, trust me . . . the Mortgage Document WILL SURFACE and in 99% of the cases the bank will PAY the back taxes and THEN get a Redemption Deed and THEN add that to the Owners mortgage as a Delinquent Payment and then file a Foreclosure suit against the owner. So either way the taxes will be paid and either way the owner will pay them or the house will be foreclosed.

So lets assume there is NO Mortgage, and you purchase the home for $25,000. Did you pay for and have a "Title Search" done, also referred to as a Title Commitment? I can assure you that 95% or more of the Investor buyer's that competed against me and my partner on the courthouse steps did NOT bother to purchase a Title Commitment. And I heard about one poor sole that by not doing so, bought a foreclosure and ALSO unknowingly bought the IRS Lien in the amount of several hundred thousand dollars. See, IRS liens are NEVER erased. Mortgages can be, but not government liens. So let's say you DID buy this house from the Land Commissioner and it had no mortgage and you did purchase a title commitment and there were no other liens and you now own the home. Sounds like a rather good investment. However, the homeowner in Arkansas will be notified by the state, that their home has been SOLD to you. Or, it might be you knocking on the door and saying "hey, just wanted to let you know that I now own your home and you have to start paying me rent of $1,200 a month or I'm going to evict you". Either way, the original owner is going to find out what happened. AND, by state law, they have "Redemption Rights" which give them at least one full year to go to the county and say "oops, here's a cashiers check for the back taxes and penalty" I owed you, in which case the county will tell you, the buyer of the Commissioner Deed, that they are sorry, but the previous owner has decided to pay the taxes . . . and enclosed is your check for $25,000 that you paid. You now Un-Own the property. Now if the home was Vacant, let's pray that you didn't make the mistake of spending $30,000 in remodeling it and renting it in the first six months of your new ownership, because now that you have been Un-Owned . . . the original owner gets to KEEP 100% of ALL the improvements as a bonus.

So the bottom line is that you cannot make any improvements or spend any money on a tax deed purchased home until all rights of redemption have expired. Now IF there are extenuating circumstances that allowed the expiration of redemption to pass and the previous owner files a lawsuit, they could very well STILL get their property back.

So as I said in the beginning, tax deed purchases can have a host of problems associated with them and unless your that rich attorney, you might get taken to the cleaners.

Now let's look at another angle because you say "Well Dave, in MY state, you can buy a tax lien or a tax deed and do so within 1 year of the delinquent tax and it's set in concrete". Ok, well, when I was a new real estate broker way back in 1973 and came across these Diamond Mine Golden Opportunities for buying tax deeds, I spent an untold amount of time searching for the right properties. I found the best one to be a parcel of land about an acre off of a main street that was about 50 feet of prime street frontage and several hundred feet back. After spending hundreds of hours on this parcel, I discovered IT DOESN'T EXIST!!!! That's right . . . there is NOTHING in the laws that say the property you purchase has to even exist! Now about now, you saying that this is ridiculous. Why would the state sell property that doesn't exist?

Consider these events. I have a good long time personal friend that asked me one day if I received my property tax bill yet because they usually have it by now. So I pulled up the tax record on her "Name" and . . . that's right . . . she OWNED NO REAL ESTATE. So I pulled up the tax record on her Street Address and low and behold, her home was deeded to someone else almost a year ago. So after printing this out and delivering it to her, she basically went ballistic. What happened is that a Title Company, in closing a sale, incorrectly transferred HER real estate deed to someone else. It took almost 5 months for her to get that correction made. In another case, I was listing a house for sale and as I always do, I pulled the tax record to make sure that the home I'm selling is actually owned by the people I'm meeting. Problem was that it was owned by a husband and wife by the name of Pete and Denise and the tax record showed Pete and Laura. So, knowing that he bought the home prior to getting married years ago, I'm thinking that his "X Wife" was probably still on the deed, HOWEVER, I'm not certain that his current wife even knows he had a previous wife, so I pull him aside and ask "now who is Laura?". He said he had no idea and never heard of a Laura _____. So assuming that he's telling me the truth, I informed the title company that his house will probably sell pretty quick and I need them to find out why Laura is on his deed and not Denise. Well, as it turned out . . . there was a George that owned a property in another county in another city, that married a "Laura" and wanted to put his wife on his deed. And believe it or not, it was the exact same street number and address, but just a different city and county. Well, I've heard that "people" make mistakes and that sometimes on rare occasions that "government workers" make mistakes. Somebody adding Laura to George's deed, pulled up the address . . . grabbed it without making sure the city and county also matched and took that deed record, which was MY Pete's house and added Laura on HIS DEED! I sold the house in 15 days and it took exactly 15 days of lightening speed, jumping through hoops to get that deed corrected having to change all the mortgages, etc. recorded.

One more example. I spend over 2,000 hours of research on the 330 acre Lake Norrell area containing 230 homes and what I did was actually pull 230 Deeds . . . extract the exact "Metes and Bounds" property description . . . feed those metes and bounds numbers into a Plot Deeding Program that actually "drew" the plat. Then I took all 230 plats and connected them together on a google area map, in color code, just like putting together a puzzle. I also built a database with every homeowner, containing the name, street address, acres, size, pictures of the homes, etc and my information database was at this point superior to the County Records. One day, a dude from California called me up and said he sees on my Lake Norrell website that I am the premier real estate go-to guy and he has 2+ acres in Lake Norrell that he wants to sell. . . . . I'm sorry . . . . I had to pause a few minutes to stop laughing here. So having impeccable, exact records by metes and bounds of EVERY parcel of land in this 330 acre lake, I can find ownership records from my database in a matter of minutes. He described his land and told me what street it was off and the shape and size and even emailed me a "photograph" he personally took when he "visited" the property. At first I was a bit confused because I had NO record of him or his transaction and the land he was describing and it's location didn't belong to him, and it fact, it didn't even exist. Now I tried my best to assure him that HIS PROPERTY DOES NOT EXIST. And he was mad enough to punch me in the face if he was in person because he Insisted that the state of Arkansas is not going to sell property that "doesn't exist". Ok . . . when you buy a Tax Deed, you are receiving a Quitclaim Deed, meaning that they are Quiting all rights and ownership interest they have, HOWEVER, they might not have any. He wasn't buying my argument. So to be a nice guy, I pulled all the details and deed metes and bounds on the area he was referring to and low and behold, after about 10 hours of research, I discovered that an elderly lady had owned about 20 acres of land on the lake for 30 something years and she passed away. Her estate sold off the 20 acres in divided "parcels" . . . with some being 1 acre, some 5 acres, etc. So when Saline County recorded all these new re-divided deeds, they "erased" and "replaced" ALL of the 20 acres of land, which I was able to find all the components of the transactions which added up to 20 acres, however the county INADVERTANTLY missed ONE parcel of land and didn't erase or replace it and therefore was showing about 2 acres left that were actually a part of two other Legal parcels. So the reason HIS property was a Delinquent Tax Deed is because (1) there was no living owner (2) the property didn't exist, therefore no one was paying tax on this non-existent parcel of land and HE bought it for $900. After I explained all this to him, he had a few chosen words for me and hung up.

So I think you get my point here. Buying Delinquent Tax Deeds have potentially lots of problems and issues, first of which . . . They Might Not Exist.

You can safely assume that there is a GOOD REASON that real estate taxes are not paid. It's a fact that nationally about 90% to 95% of all delinquent tax bills are eventually paid by the original owner, which only leaves you with about 5% left to pursue. A certain number of those aren't going to exist and a certain number are going to have government liens and a certain number are going to be PAID for by the mortgagee holding a mortgage interest (their not stupid), and the few that are left are being pursued by large corporate expert attorneys that are not looking to make a killing in buying and reselling the land BUT rather buying the Lien and reselling their Lien at a higher price OR getting a 8% to 18% return on allowed "Interest" for the time they held the lien.

So with all that long winded explanation about Tax Deeds, please don't waste your time and effort pursuing such property and don't pay for courses or subscriptions for a "list" of these jewels.

Now there ARE real deals out there that IF you happen to come across one, don't just close your eyes to it. I was all set to buy two parcels in Lake Norrell with two cabins on them owned by a woman thought to live in another county. After watching them for about a year, I was about 30 days from making a purchase, when all of a sudden a brother, a local "politician" must have got wind and paid the tax current. I was fully aware though, that getting these Tax Deeds, the original owner still had another 12 Months to "redeem" the deed, meaning that if during the next 12 months they decide to take their property back, all they have to pay me is the amount I paid. I just wasn't going to make any improvements and hope that no one noticed I bought them.

# LESSON #7

## HOW DO YOU FIND "OTHER" SPECIAL SITUATIONS?

It's like looking for a needle in a haystack. You've got to do your homework. In addition to the foreclosure properties from their various sources, be mindful of special situations at all times.

You have to remain Open-Minded about deals and not get too focused that they have to be a "foreclosure." Tell your friends, relatives, acquaintances and business associates, title company representative, real estate agent, etc. that you're on the hunt for "troubled real estate". That's the number one source for leads. And don't forget that a Property Owner Association Board Member also usually knows "who's" in trouble in their subdivision because they're not paying the POA dues. So either get on your board, or become friends with a board member.

In the summer time, drive around the areas you like. ANY house that looks to be in BAD shape physically, OR the grass is out of control . . . write down the address, pull the tax record, pull the Deed and Mortgage record. Do <u>your</u> unique (CSI) Comprehensive Search Investigator job.

You can also make arrangements with a local title company that you'll always do your closings with them, in exchange, if they'll pull your title searches, also referred to as "Title Commitments". They should be able to do it for $50 to $75 and some will do it free if your giving them business. It almost goes without saying you need a title search before you enter into a bid or purchase agreement. Reason being is that you might buy a foreclosure that has a huge IRS lien attached and once you buy the house . . . YOU now also own that nice lien and it now becomes your problem to pay the IRS. You could easily get whipped out.

Investing in foreclosed houses can be compared to the stock market. Buying stock would be like buying a basic house to live in. Buying a foreclosure can be like buying commodities . . . you might loose more than your original investment!! So make sure you know what you're doing before you jump in. The best advise if you haven't been in the market before is (1) Stay very close to home. Invest only in your town and the areas you know more about. (2) Once you identify a possible property, pull the tax record and see what that reveals. (3) Get to know a good real estate agent and stay in constant contact with them by phone, email, FaceBook . . . so they DON'T forget in their day to day hustle to call you if something looks good. (4) Make sure you establish a relationship with a bank, or better a local Credit Union. Make sure you have your financial arrangements in place that are just as good as paying cash. (5) And use your (CSI) Comprehensive Search Investigation methods to find out everything you can.

Another good source for homes is Burned-Out-Want-A-Be-Investors. In other words, there are people that at one point in time thought it would be a great idea to buy homes to rent. They bought in the lower income bracket and have had a Come-To-Jesus meeting on the realization that "Renting is just not for me". They're tired of the tenants moving out every time the X Boyfriend starts shooting the house up, breaking the windows to get in, not paying the rent and the headaches of evictions, the damage done by tenants, neighbor complaints about the Trailer Trash Renters they have, and just WANT OUT! If they're managing the property themselves and they've owned it for more than 2 years, they are a prime candidate. So search the tax records in an area you might want to buy in and search by "Subdivision". Scan through each home and pick out all the ones that the Owner Address is different than the Tax Bill Mailing Address. That indicates a rented house. Then do a Reverse Address Search and see who the name of the person is with a telephone there. If it's NOT the Owner of the house then that also indicates a Renter. Then do a tax record search on the Owner name and see how many homes they own. If they own 7 or so homes then you KNOW they are in the rental business. Then pull and record THEIR information as to Home Address, Full Name, Wife's Name, Telephone Number. Then see if you can find them on FaceBook. Get all the info you can. KEEP ALL THIS INFO for future use in case they don't want to sell now but might later. Drive by EACH one of his properties and see what kind of landlord he appears to be. Do the houses look rundown? If so, he's probably a slumlord and getting tired of the business. Once you have enough research on this guy, mail him a letter or message him on facebook and tell him that you are an investor looking to buy some rental property and got his name from somebody as a person that might be interested in selling a rent house. IF you get a positive response . . . then from that point, you're only talking about "negotiation".

I have a couple of guys that after 7 years with 4 houses told me DUMP THEM . . . . sell them for whatever you can get even it's for only what my mortgage balance is. I'm Done. I'm finished! I've had it!

You can also watch the local paper for Divorce Filings and Obituaries. On the divorce filings, try to find the name in the reverse lookup websites and look up the house in the tax record and if it looks like it might be the priced house in your search criteria, mail a letter to the Occupant. Sometimes neither spouse wants to live in the house and many times they MUST sell to distribute the property and you'll be getting to them BEFORE it reaches the point they hire a real estate agent to sell. And the same for the Obituaries . . . . Pick up the names of the "nearest" relative or survivors in the notice and do your CSI research to see if the house is now occupied by one surviving spouse or is it now vacant. There will be a probate in most cases, so see if you can find a relative to inquire about buying the house IF it fits your buying criteria after looking at the tax record information.

Bottom line . . . be open minded. Always think in terms of "where" can I find a house. The more you think about it, it will be driven in your subconscious mind and you'll do pretty good finding prospective investments.

Also, meet with your new Realtor friend every now and then for lunch and give him a written search criteria you'd like him to look up for you. Let's say you're looking for homes that are in the $10,000 to $50,000 price range in certain neighborhoods. What you want is for him/her to search the MLS system for all "Expired Listings" between $10K and $50K in that neighborhood that went Off the Market more than 1 year ago. The MLS searching allows most agents to search by entering a Subdivision Name or even "drawing a polygon" on a map of the area they want to search. What you want is for him to email you ALL the Detail Listing Information Sheets for all those homes. Once he emails you those listings, you can search the Tax Record pretty quickly to see IF that house has had a sale SINCE that listing expired. Trash that one. But if it still has the same ownership, start your research on that house. Determine the current value, potential value, drive by, and contact that owner in one of several ways. Either by telephone, writing or knocking on the door and saying you were interested in buying a house in this area and knew they had their home for sale last year, or whenever and wanted to know if they would still be willing to sell and talk about "price". If they invite you in, you'll find out all about why they want to sell, price, you'll see all the things that need to be fixed, etc. and you leave by saying you'll get back to them and be sure to get their email address OR just start negotiating a price.

So let's do a Summary Recap on the various types of "Properties" to always be mindful of and keeping your eyes and ears open for:

- ➜ (1) Foreclosures from HUD website
- ➜ (2) Foreclosures from real estate agents
- ➜ (3) Foreclosures direct from Bank information
- ➜ (4) Foreclosures from a paid "list" or monthly subscription
- ➜ (5) Vacant homes
- ➜ (6) Neighbor referrals of troubled homes, situations, vacancies
- ➜ (7) Search for Renter Owners in the tax records
- ➜ (8) Have one or two real estate agents searching and stay in contact with them
- ➜ (9) Watch for Divorce or Obituary notifications
- ➜ (10) Give your agent a "criteria" to search for old expired listing

You will find that the more you do investigations of potential property, the faster you'll get. So, let's touch briefly on ORGANIZATION of information gathered. The longer you search and the more property you search, the more information you will gather that becomes discombobulated and disorganized and you don't want that to happen, because 9 out of 10 times, there will be a super deal pop up that you remember researching some 2 years ago and YOU didn't keep the FILE!

Here's how I organize my files. You should put ALL of your information in a Documents Folder if using Windows based computers. Mac has it's own built in easy methods. Within the Document folder, name a folder "(1) INVESTMENT PROPERTY". Now there's a reason for the "(1)" before the folder name . . . . because it will be at the top of the window when you open it. And putting in all caps will stand out better among other files in the folder. Next within the investment folder number EACH property you perform ANY investigative work on at all, and name them as "Easy St-1234", "Long Ln-1818", etc. In other words, you are naming the folder in automatic alphabetic order by having the street name first followed by the street number. This way, once your file reaches hundreds of searches going back years, if you come across an address that you think you investigated before . . . you can find it in seconds. Within the Easy St-1234 folder, number all the documents you put in the folder, such as (1) Tax Record (2) Tax Bill (3) Aerial View (4) Location Map (5) Deed (6) Mortgage (7) Owner Info Sheet, etc. You get the gist here. The REASON you number them is because you know that each document in this folder is in Chronological order as you created it. So if you have (25) Tax Record, that tells you that you did one way back there and have another one labeled number 25. That could be 2 years apart. NEVER throw anything away as far as computer records in your files. And any hard copies of documents that you've gathered in your research . . . . scan them . . . and put them IN the proper folder. Below is a picture of my document folder.

# LESSON #7

## HOW TO BUY BEFORE THE FORECLOSURE!

Keep your ear to the ground. Earlier I sited an actual example where my partner and I purchased the lake house direct from the owner prior to him getting foreclosed on. I've contacted many an owner to discuss how I might be able to help them and most won't answer the door or telephone or even a note left on the door. Only about 5% will communicate with you because they're embarrassed and/or in a state of denial thinking they can fix the problem and don't need your help. But it's always worth that try. I've told you about several "real" examples about quick turnaround profit deals, but did I tell you HOW MANY I chased before I found them? No . . . But let's just understand that working full time in the real estate business and looking for "deals" in an entire year . . . I might find 2 or 3. So they're there . . . just not easy to find. But this will also depend on just how big your market is and what the foreclosure rate is at the time.

You have to continue to be persistent though. You have to keep trying to make contact and get in their door at their home to discuss how you might be able to help. Of course to them helping means your going to loan them the money (a perfect stranger) so they can catch the mortgage up, but to you, helping means possibly buying their house and preventing a foreclosure on their record and saving their credit. That's a wide wide gap there in thinking. I have heard of investors buying a house from a potential foreclosure victim and then renting the house to them for the amount of the payment they were making. I wouldn't discount that idea.

Let's assume you have a foreclosure list or access to one on a regular basis. Pick the houses by location that you might be interested in looking at and start doing your basic research, namely the CMA to determine what it might sell for, getting the owner's telephone number and trying to contact them and determine how many mortgages they have and for how much. If it looks like a deal might be in the making then get your Title Search done and then work on doing a "D&D" or Down & Dirty Analysis to see how much you'd be willing to offer, taking into consideration all the costs involved. More about the D&D later.

Then you contact that owner direct and if they're in that 5%, you might just strike a deal and even give them a thousand or so to boot to sell and move out.

I've previously discussed many ways to find other property as well but concentrating specifically on the "Pre-Foreclosure" you need a good "angle". You need a good "reason" for contacting them, so think out your plan in advance. You might spend some time drafting a really good letter to mail to them and your time might be spent wiser. If they call from that letter, then you're already in a good position to get to the meat of a possible transaction.

# LESSON #8

## A WORD ABOUT PROPERTY INSURANCE

When you buy an investment house, whether it be a special situation house or a foreclosure, you have to purchase homeowners insurance regardless. Keep in mind the premiums will be about 4 times higher than that for a home you live in, if the house is vacant and investment property. That adds up fast. So shop around and make sure you find a GOOD Insurance Agent willing to work with you that wants your business. I found that if you go on-line and do a search for best Homeowner Insurance companies, you'll find several sites that you fill in the basic information and you'll get tons of excellent price quotes. Do this for your PERSONAL home and in the process of discussions, tell them you are also looking into buying investment property and just how good a deal can they make on that too. The more business you give them the better your overall rates will be. Later in the Down & Dirty Analysis section, we'll discuss more about how to account for these costs.

So if you don't already have a good insurance agent, do some calling and checking and find out who has the least expensive homeowners insurance for a vacant house. And please, don't think that just because you know your agent well or it's a relative that you have the best possible deal. The rates are NOT in the control of your agent but rather the Insurance Company that they have to represent. And don't even <u>consider</u> being untruthful telling your insurance company you're going to live in the house or that it's rented if it's not. If you have a major loss like a fire and they find out, your entire claim will be denied and that could cost you dearly.

# LESSON #9

## WHAT IS TITLE INSURANCE AND DO YOU NEED IT?

Title Insurance is a NECESSITY in the foreclosure business and believe it or not, most people I know don't buy it when they purchase a foreclosure. Now I'm referring to CASH purchases on the courthouse steps type foreclosures. All other purchases like a HUD or Bank foreclosure, you'll be getting a Mortgage and it's a requirement to have Title Insurance. It's a huge risk that I would never take on a courthouse step purchase.

Title insurance simply insures the title and the rights that go with that assurance. In other words when you buy title insurance, the insurance company is guaranteeing you that you have clear title or clear ownership, free and clear of any and all liens, only subject to what is noted, if anything, in the title policy which you find out about when you do a title search. When you establish a relationship with a Title Company for all your business, you might need to refer to buying a "Title Commitment" on prospective property. Because you're not actually BUYING any insurance, but rather you're just paying for the "search" they have to do to enable them to Issue you a Title Policy.

On any foreclosure, there could be multiple potential liens and claims against the property you're buying. And if those claims are not known to you, then you could be unknowingly assuming the responsibility to pay them. For example, lets say a 1st mortgage exist on a home in the amount of $90,000. And the value of the home should be around $120,000 and the house is in good shape. The house is in the foreclosure listings and you talk to the owner direct and make a deal to purchase the house for all cash, outside of the foreclosure. You purchase the house and pay all cash from a Line of Credit you got at your bank, which is not a real estate loan. You close and don't purchase title insurance to save the $300 or so cost. You do your fix up and put the house up for sale and discover you have a 2nd mortgage on your house in the amount of $20,000. You've been had. You assumed that mortgage unknowingly and now will most likely lose hard cash on this transaction. Only a title search would have revealed that.

Had you purchased a Title Search which is the prerequisite to issuing Title Insurance from your friendly title company for $50 or $75, you'd have known there was a 2nd mortgage and wouldn't have bought the house to begin with. When you do buy a title search, generally, the title company will give you credit for the amount paid when you purchase the title insurance policy.

Now let's suppose you're buying a regular foreclosure and you DO purchase a title search and there are several liens on the property. IF you've bought the house on the court house steps all other liens are erased and you own the property free and clear of all liens. Of course you also now purchased Title Insurance at the closing of the purchase. Now you've fixed the house and you've sold it and the title company has since discovered a claim for $15,000 against your property. Good thing you have title insurance, because the title company now has to get that lien removed through legal actions and will be liable to pay it off for you. The key word in a foreclosure that cleared all those liens is "Noticed Up" . . . that is, all the liens that were found were noticed up about the foreclosure process and those liens were all erased, BUT, if the title search missed a legitimate lien and didn't properly notice up that lien holder, then the lien could still be valid, BUT, you're not liable for it . . . they are!! I'm not providing "Legal Advise" here . . . only my personal knowledge based on my actual experiences.

When dealing in risky foreclosure property, you always want to purchase a title search before purchasing and purchase title insurance when you do buy the property. That little amount of money can save you a bunch.

# LESSON #10

## LET'S TALK ABOUT "REHAB", "REPAIRS"

When you're buying a foreclosure or a special situation house, it is very important to get inside the house if at all possible and determine just how much you might have to spend to get the house ready for reselling. You don't want to be tossing dice.

Buying a courthouse step foreclosure is buying <u>sight unseen</u>, and "<u>as is</u>" and there is no guarantee of clear title, ie the IRS. You can get a clean title by buying title insurance, but the sight unseen and "as is", is up to you to investigate properly. Put that CSI hat on. Your first approach is to try to contact the owner occupant that is being foreclosed on, and get in the door to see the inside. Once you've made a walk though and sat down and talked with them about what's broken, you'll have a good idea what to fix and how much to allow for that expense. If you can't get inside or the house and is vacant, you can walk around and maybe peek in some windows. Many times you'll find the house has been breached . . . a window or door is open and even though your technically "trespassing", there's really no harm in walking in and looking around for a few minutes.

Otherwise your taking a gamble . . . your plan here is to purchase the house at the court house steps . . . . then immediately (like IN LESS THAN AN HOUR) go to the house and inform the previous owner occupant that YOU have just purchased this house at foreclosure and IF they don't let you in to discuss the subject of them moving, you will call the sheriff and have them evicted and thrown out on the street. Harsh words, but you've got to make an impression to get inside. Once inside you can make your repairs determination. In the case where the house is vacant, call a locksmith, tell him you just bought this house at foreclosure and show him your paperwork you have, if asked, and have him open the door and make a key to the current lock. Don't change the key or the lock at this point. Keep in mind . . . you haven't "PAID" for this house yet and the deed is not IN your name yet . . . you're operating on the assumption that you're fixing to pay for it and going to be the owner.

As a side note here, I once spoke at a Nothing Down Seminar as a Keynote Speaker regarding how to "manage" rental property. About 2/3rds through the talk I asked for any questions and the first question was from a very intelligent guest that asked "Isn't a lot of this stuff you're telling us Against The Law?". I said, "well, it may very well be, but I'm not causing anyone any harm in the way I go about this and I'm just cutting through the red tape like the shortest distance between two points being a Straight Line. I've done this for 20 years and never had a problem." So if you're starting to think . . . ummm, I'm going to have to check to see if that's LEGAL here in my state . . . just consider if it's illegal in your state, it's probably also illegal in my state but if the government put everyone in jail that broke any kind of law no matter how insignificant, we'd ALL be in jail. So you use your best judgement.

So back to getting in the house. Once inside, if you're satisfied, then you head to the foreclosure agents office and perform their closing to complete the purchase and give them a cashier's check for the amount you successfully bided for. If you're not satisfied with the house, you can usually call the foreclosure agent and tell them you are **NOT** going to come in and close. You can probably only do this a few times. If you make a habit of being the winning bidder and then don't close, they will Black Ball you from bidding in the future. So be prepared to buy sight unseen and just allow for the risk in your Down & Dirty Analysis for repairs.

As for the Non-Foreclosure, Distressed Other type homes, you still MUST get inside to see the extent of the damage and repairs. Your WORSE nightmare is that hidden downstairs, is a half-inch of Nasty Black Mold that gives you the instant creepers and makes you feel like you're breathing deadly toxic air! I once went into an abandoned home in a very nice neighborhood that was all brick and from the outside looked like a possible jewel. But once inside, WOW . . . the AC unit was in the attic of this 1-story home and it must have been on and leaking water for a good year or so. Why power would be on in a vacant home, I have no idea, but water leakage was very evident in every room of the house and there was literally "Black Mold" growing up ALL the interior walls of the home 4 feet from the floor. It was just like HAIR growing on a wall. If you moved quickly, the "hair" moved. It was very scary! I immediately left and called an Environmental Company friend of mine that took a quick look and told me this was about the worst he's ever seen and it would costs about $15,000 to $20,000 to "remediate". KEEP IN MIND . . . when you fix up a house to sell, regardless what was wrong and what you fixed, you still have a obligation to "Disclose" any prior dangerous situations that you corrected. As a Realtor, it's a LAW. Failure to "Disclose" any pertinent information an agent might have about a home they're selling could cost them their real estate license and career. But if you're just a average person buying directly from the owner or bank and no agents are involved, there are generally NO LAWS that a seller has to "disclose", however, common sense will tell you . . . IF there was something dangerous and a neighbor tells the new homeowner about it, there's a good chance the seller will be SUED if they did not disclose. People can sue anyone for any reason. Even though there might not be a specific law that you had to disclose it, do you want to take the chance that a Judge "Legislates from the Bench" and rescinds the sale and fines you? Not to mention the fact you might WIN the lawsuit . . . great news right? Well, I guess so, if you consider paying $25,000 in legal fees to win, right?

So, how do you "assess" repairs? How do you determine what needs to be done? Well, I can assure you, unless you've been in the business of remodeling or rehabbing and reselling homes, you might be way off base on what YOU think needs to be done vs what you SHOULD do. I talked with a nice guy from California a few years ago that bought a sight-unseen foreclosure that had been victim to a small fire. He bought the house dirt cheap before he ever actually saw it. He never did really tell me for sure that he's EVER seen the house in Little Rock, but he had hired some people to fix it up and wanted to know if I would sell it for him. Well, he was in a very very bad area, not to mention the "average" sale price of homes in this small subdivision was about $16,000. I think he said he ONLY paid like $12,000 for the house. A STEAL by all "California" standards since it would probably be worth $200,000 in CA. But once I found out that he'd spent around $15,000 fixing the house up including GRANITE COUNTERS in the kitchen, I thought MAN . . . you're NUTS! He's wanting to sell a house for $75,000+ in a neighborhood with average sales of $16,000. I couldn't tell from the phone if he just had a bad cold or was CRYING when I broke the news. I told him, I could sell it, but doubt he'd get anymore than $18,000 and that people in that neighborhood don't even know what granite counters are. He decided I wasn't the right agent for the job.

So the bottom line is you have to KNOW what improvements to make, depending on what type neighborhood you're in. I've seen foreclosures that were really torn up in $500,000+ neighborhoods that the rehabber put in Cheap Mobile Home quality carpets, Home Depot PERGO flooring, calling that "wood" and FORMICA countertops in the kitchen. SERIOUSLY? You just shaved off about $150,000 to $200,000 of the value off that home. Rehab accordingly. If you don't know what a Good Home should look like in a particular neighborhood . . . it's EASY to find out. Call any real estate agent and tell them you want to see about 5 to 8 homes in that subdivision . . . that you're thinking of buying a home there. I know . . . that's dirty . . . that's a terrible thing to do, but agents have to deal with all kinds and pretty much get use to it and besides, IF you plan to buy a house in that neighborhood, you can use one of the agents you chose to spend the time to show you around. But the fact that you looked at 8 homes in the neighborhood for sale, and you have all the MLS Listing sheets, you KNOW about what the home has to look like for a particular price. If you can't see why one appears to be priced way too low or too high, ask that agent and I'm sure they can give you an insight as to why.

As a rule of thumb, when I buy a $40,000 rehab house, I don't expect to spend any more than $2,800. And on a $100,000 about $5,000 to $7,000. On a $150,000 home, about the same. In my area, the majority of homes that would be considered "good" areas of town have a Average selling price of around $175,000. That being the case, I NEVER buy a house less than $18,000 and I NEVER buy a house more than $180,000. Reason being is that you are getting "outside" the "majority" of the Buyer Pool. There might be for example an average of 100 homes a month sold in all of the "good" areas of town as a total. Of those, 10% will be less than $40,000 and 10% will be more than $250,000. So the majority of buyers will be between around $60,000 to $175,000, so try to also keep the "resale" after your rehab WITHIN THE RANGE OF THE MAJORITY SALES IN THAT CITY. Again, if you don't know these Averages, your Realtor agent can tell you that almost off the top of their head if they've been in the business for several years.

Now there are some other dire cautions such as Termites, Hidden Damage, Home Inspections and Insurance. As for Termites, there are many places in the country that termites can destroy a house and Arkansas is one of them. Termites can eat 1 foot of wood a day. So if you're in a termite prone area, you MUST get termite insurance at the time you buy the house. But how do you check to see if you have termites without spending any money? Simple. Pick a termite company your currently doing business with or one you plan to use a lot. Give them a call and tell them you are Fixing to Purchase a house at 123 Easy Street next week or 15 days from now and you need a BID for a Termite Policy because you are going to use them for ALL the properties you bid. Ok . . . they CANNOT give you a BID site unseen. They have to go out to the house . . . inspect it as best they can, even if they can't get inside and determine by their expert servicemen if there is any current damage. Once they give you a Bid, it will either be a "all clear" on termites and the price is $X OR it will contain a surprise that you have EXTENSIVE damage that will cost $5,000 and then the annual policy will be the same $X a year. So . . . you now have a good hard estimate. As for "Hidden Damage", if you're experienced in remodeling and rehabbing, you have a gut feeling when you're CSI'ing the house. Otherwise you NEED TO HIRE A HOME INSPECTOR and cough up the $450 or so dollars to have them do a fairly detailed inspection. Now on a home that is Listed by a Realtor, HUD or other Foreclosure, it's never a problem getting a Home Inspection, but my advise here is to make an OFFER on the house first and make sure you get the price you want, SUBJECT TO Inspections, etc. and THEN hire the Home Inspector. If everything checks out ok or nothing that you didn't know or expect then you proceed to a closing, otherwise you cancel the sale and you're out $450. As for Insurance . . . keep in mind, that a "specific home" might cost DOUBLE the insurance premium as the house next door that is identical. That's right. If a home was subject to several fires or several pipes busting and causing a flood, that could drive the price of insurance up on THAT home up significantly. This information can be obtained by getting a C.L.U.E. Report (Comprehensive Loss Underwriting Exchange) when possible. The CLUE reports are a central clearing house of all insurance claims filed. An insurance company can take the liberty of charging a premium based on what that report says. You CANNOT pull a CLUE report on line for any home other than your own unless you have some vested interest, but you DO need to tell your Insurance Agent that you want a Solid QUOTE on an insurance premium on the home you're considering purchasing in advance. And just to be safe, ask them IF they pulled the CLUE report so you don't get hit with a last minute surprise at closing.

So, in summary, use as a rough guide not to spend any more than around 7% of the purchase price for "repairs". Don't over-class the improvements for that neighborhood and don't under-class them either. Only buy within the range of homes selling in the "majority" of the Buyer Pool for that area.

There are always exceptions to the rule and there is always SOMEBODY in a neighborhood that has to be the "highest" sale, but you need to have a gut-feeling and some good experience to know when you take on that risk.

Now this would be an appropriate time to touch on some off-the-grid type property, or property you might say is not the typical large volume foreclosure property. Here I'm referring to Rural Property. That's almost a totally different animal. Generally if your going to be working in a Rural area, you're not going to have very many foreclosures but you might come across some distressed situations. That being said, one would also assume that you most likely also live in a rural area and understand things like Perk Test, Septic Testing, Flood Plains, and Environmental Considerations.

In other words, you might come across a rural piece of property that was foreclosed on that was a nice little 3 Bedroom sitting on 10 acres that seems to be a diamond in the rough. But there happens to be a Hog Farm up the hillside and that, how shall we say, poo poo, has saturated the ground and contaminated the well drinking water. Or you might be in a low lying area that a septic system won't perk and your sewage won't drain properly. These are all too uncommon types of property to go into any detail on but if you're working with a local Real Estate Agent that deals in rural property, you'll most likely have someone watching your back for pitfalls that come with Rural Property.

# LESSON #11

## HOW DO YOU DETERMINE RE-SELL VALUE?

I am "Plugged In" to a neighborhood that has about 500 homes. The average sale price is around $175,000. RARELY is there a home in this subdivision that sells for $150,000 or less unless it's a foreclosure, torn the hell up or very very small, which in itself would be rare. And there are only about 20 sales that are over $200,000 in the last 5 years. BUT, I also know the "heartbeat" of the neighborhood. I know that more owners are "remodeling" their homes to live more comfortably or for a sale in the near future, opposed to a so called "declining" neighborhood where the prices are going down.

What this means is that it's a fairly safe bet to buy on the high side and spend "good money" for the Extras and you'll get your money back in this subdivision. That is the kind of information that a Realtor knows that the general public DOESN'T know, and not even the average homeowner in the subdivision knows. I know one home in particular that had a county value of $170,000 where the homeowner spent $100,000 in remodeling that the county is not even aware of. The 40 year old home now looks "BETTER" than a brand new home. It appraised for $260,000 and if the owner was of mind to sell, they wouldn't take a dime less and they'd get it. Determined, Proud owners in a subdivision are what drives the prices up in a subdivision.

Now as a Realtor, and a real estate broker of 43 years, I can tell you right now I meet people all the time that have some pretty wild ideas of what a house should sell for. If they own the house, they love it and they think everyone will too. In other words, they're "married to their home". That doesn't make it more valuable. You CANNOT use Zillow.com to determine Value! You CANNOT use Trulia. com to determine Value! You CANNOT use any website that takes the "average" of an "area" that doesn't even confine itself to the like-kind homes and arrive at Value. You CANNOT even rely on an Appraiser to tell you the "best" price to sell. The ONLY reliable source to determine "what will my house sell for" is a Real Estate Agent. And of all agents, only about 60% of them are going to give you a TRUTHFUL "Hand-on-the-Bible" value. The other 40% want to make a FAST sale and will give you a low ball price OR they will "agree" with whatever WILD number you come up with just to get the listing, KNOWING that after 6 months or so you'll realize that "maybe" you're price is to high and your need to come down. So find the right agent. Find that agent you trust. Find that agent that seems to be Honest. Find that agent that's been in the business for at least 3 years and Find that agent that is **not** the Top Producer that doesn't have time for you.

So, unless you're in the real estate business, you're going to have to develop a relationship with a real estate agent and have them provide you with a CMA (Comparative Market Analysis) whenever you need one, at a very low costs or for free. If you know the agent well and you plan to do business with him/her or refer them clients for doing a good job, then you can probably get this information free. You can't look in a crystal ball for your value. At the least, find out from an agent what the "average price per square foot" is for homes selling in certain neighborhoods. I have clients that know that homes sell for $100 per foot in "their" neighborhood and then when they see a house selling for $50 per foot somewhere . . . they actually think it's a BARGAIN! Well, that neighborhood might sell on average for $42 per foot . . . so be smart. And when you get ready to Sell, consider using this agent and push for a good discount in their standard percentage. I know agents in markets that charge 6% that will do it for 3% or 4% and there are a lot of companies that are Discount Brokers that serve no purpose OTHER THAN to put your property in the Realtors MLS System for a one-time Flat Fee. They won't even be in your state. You do all the work. You take the pictures and email to them and they put you in the MLS. When a Realtor calls to show the house, their 1-800 number actually "Forwards" to YOUR phone to set up the showing. And you'll negotiate with that Buyer Agent direct, saving at least 1/2 the normal commission on a sale.

You can check around and do your own analysis, but again, unless you're in the business, you could be way off the mark on value and you don't want that to happen on a house you're buying to resell. And if you DO plan to rely on Zillow or Trulia to determine the "value" of a house . . . you might just as well call your local psychic. I'd place my money on the psychic.

# LESSON #12

## HOW TO YOU DETERMINE WHAT TO PAY?

Again, the same as with Selling a home, you have to use the same exact considerations for what to buy the house for, except when you're buying, you're looking for that "Bargain" which means there is "something" wrong with it and you need someone capable of knowing how to "discount" from "average" sale price what that house <u>should</u> be bought for. Now keep in mind that the SELLER pays for the commission to sell a house, so by you having a Buyer Agent represent you, the commission is FREE to you. So make good use of that information stream. A note of Caution: If I spend the time showing you homes and doing a lot of FREE Research for you and I find out you bought a house through ANOTHER Agent . . . I'm DONE with you! Don't even bother to call me again. If you'll be loyal to me, I'll be loyal and work for you. That's the way that works.

Now as an Investor, you have other motives. Your motive is probably not to buy and live in the house. You need to buy at a discount, spend money on Repairs, pay for Utilities while you're doing this work, know who to hire to do the work that doesn't cost an arm and a leg and take other costs into consideration like Insurance, Realtor Selling Costs, fees on the purchase and fees on the resell. All that is part of the whole picture. Sometimes you get TOO EXCITED about a house and you don't think logically about all these cost and whether or not it's really a good FINANCIAL deal or not, so I created a quick excel spreadsheet I call my Down & Dirty to make that quick, non-emotional "just the numerical facts" analysis.

As my best wealthy investor always said . . ."You can lie about the numbers . . . but the numbers don't lie". I go into more detail about the Down and Dirty in Lesson #14. But for now, just know that you MUST have a Realtor involved to identify the "Best Possible" prospective properties for you and then YOU put on your CSI hat and use your Customized Down and Dirty sheet to see if you want to go to the next step in purchasing a property.

# LESSON #13

## WHAT ARE THE COURTHOUSE STEPS?

I've talked a lot about the "Court House Steps". So exactly what is that? To my knowledge, virtually all counties in the country handle foreclosure actions at their county courthouse. You have to appear personally at the court house. And most all courthouses will have a designated area where the foreclosure sales take place. Most of them are in a room or veranda area but some may actually take place on the steps leading inside. When a homeowner is in default on their payments, the lending institution hires an attorney to file a foreclosure action. Those actions will in most cases take about 2 to 3 months, but can take up to 6 months or a year. There are some large legal outfits that specialize in foreclosure services and do nothing but that. They most likely have an office in the same city as the county courthouse. They are hired by the mortgagee (foreclosing bank) and will not provide any helpful information to anyone but their client, the mortgage company, so don't count on them being friendly or helpful.

In my area, foreclosure sales take place on every Tuesday at 11:00 a.m. and a representative of the foreclosure firm appears and reads the rules of bidding quickly and then starts reading off the list of homes to be foreclosed. If a home you were planning to bid on was not called out, chances are it was worked out or delayed to another date without notice. He will start the bidding process by telling you the street address of the property and the mortgage company filing the action and then he will start by stating that ABC Bank starts with an Opening Bid of $X. This is basically the amount of their mortgage. You can count on 80% or more of these starting mortgagee bids to be in excess of the maximum amount you were willing to bid to begin with . . . along with everyone else in the room. Then the auctioneer, if your will, will ask if there are any other bids? If not, he will say, going once . . . going twice . . . . SOLD to ABC Bank in the amount of $X. Generally you will only get to bid on about 1 in 10 of the properties because the opening mortgagee bid will be in excess of the amount you were going to bid and it's too high, and then you'll also have competitive bidders on others that will quickly bid above your predetermined maximum. That's why developing a good method of contacting the owner before the foreclosure will produce more productive results if you can get in. Because you will know just how much above that mortgage is safe to bid. It's also very helpful IF you can find out what that "mortgage opening bid" is going to be.

Don't count on the legal company handing the foreclosure. They are too busy and don't give a flip about you. IF you're lucky enough to have a "friend" there, they will email you the "BID" amount which could save you an unnecessary trip to the court house. I had such a friend at the time we were doing a lot of bidding. Your only other method is to pull the county mortgage record which can most likely be done on-line in many counties, and use an amortization program to calculate what the balance of the mortgage would be FROM the date it was initiated. Otherwise you'll have to make a trip to the County Court house. You'll also have to have a saved file of "mortgage interest rates" for all periods of time, which you can get from various places on-line like BankRate.com, or do a Google search for "what was the home interest rate on April 18, 2001?" ie. Then use that rate in your computation to determine the approximate mortgage balance. THEN add about $5,000 to $10,000 on top of your number to allow for all the delinquent interest fees, attorney fees, etc. that the lender will be paying out for this foreclosure to take place. If you wind up with an estimated mortgage of $72,000 on a $75,000 house, then don't waste your time going to the auction to bid.

Another KEY item to watch for on these foreclosures is to see IF you might be interested in doing a Down & Dirty research on by LOOKING FOR the date of the original mortgage. Many legal firms doing foreclosures use the "Year" as part of their "Case Number", for example a home with an original mortgage in 1989 might have a case number like LRK1989-254686, where those first four numbers are the YEAR in which the mortgage was taken out. THAT would be one to research further, opposed to one that was LRK2012-254861, which means the mortgage was taken out in 2012 and if we're in year 2014 . . . there is NO WAY there could be any equity worth bidding on unless there was a substantial down payment made, but my experience is that homes with significant down payments don't get foreclosed on. If the owner was in trouble, they'd sell.

# LESSON #14

## HOW TO SET UP YOUR DOWN & DIRTY ANALYSIS

I set my Down and Dirty analysis up in an excel spreadsheet, and each time I have a new investment to research, I open one and just "save as" and change the Name and Associated Numbers. Each one is different. Sometimes I have to add a section in the case of a client that might want to be renting, others are strictly FLIP houses for short term and others might take 4 to 6 months to fix and resell. All the factors that need to be taken into consideration don't take long to revise.

The key is to always have a "Basic" format set up that you always open and use to revise and then SAVE AS another name so as to preserve your original custom D&D. NOTE: ALWAYS CALCULATE THE TRANSACTION AS "ALL CASH". When you start taking into consideration "leverage" through financing, you will NOT have an apple to apple comparison to make a good decision. The Cost of money is naturally a factor but that will vary from one investor to another. The Information that you'll need to gather BEFORE you can insert them into the D&D are basically the following:

- ▶ What's the date of projected purchase

- ▶ What is the current projected ReSell Price (from Realtor)

- ▶ What is the expected Purchase Price

- ▶ Once it's purchased, what is the estimated cost of Homeowners Insurance

- ▶ Once purchased, what will the Closing Cost & Title Insurance be

- ▶ What is the status of the Real Estate Tax, do you have to pay any back tax

- ▶ How long to you expect the rehab to take

- ▶ What is your projection for cost of Utilities: water, gas, electric for that timeframe

- ▶ What is a Termite Policy going to cost

- ▶ What will be the Closing Cost on Selling (at a higher price)

- ▶ Will there be a Realtor's commission on a resell and how much

- ▶ What Rehab work will there be and Specific breakdown of the costs

- ▶ If it's going to be rented . . . What will the Rental Rate be

**NOTE: IF YOU WILL SEND ME AN EMAIL AND REQUEST AN ACTUAL
EXCEL TEMPLATE, I'LL EMAIL MINE FOR FREE!!!**
This email address will be good until I'm either dead or in a nursing home
dbonweb@aol.com

Below is a sample Customized D&D, Down & Dirty analysis I randomly picked from the past on a deal we passed on and did not purchase. As you can see, the Percentage Return is good for a FLIP but this client was going to Rent and that would have him in the hole. Personally I would have done this deal as a easy FLIP and used that money for another project to rent.

I think the nail in the coffin on this deal was that in actuality, my client didn't realize he was going to be hit with a 20% minimum down payment of $15,000 and was thinking more like 5% down. That happens many times. Don't be shy with your real estate agent and dance around a real problem, just say you have the cash or money, BUT, you have it tied up or committed on other projects right now and can't move it.

Now WHERE did I get some of these numbers?. The square feet comes from the best source you have, which is the Tax Record. The Resale Amount comes from your CMA (Comparable Market Analysis) from your real estate agent, on what the property should sell for, in a very good condition after your repairs are made. The Maximum Offering Price is the last number you'll enter, so skip that for now. The Discount of purchase to value is simply the difference between the ReSale Amount and the Maximum Offering Price and the % number to the right of it is the Discount amount divided by the Maximum Offering Price. You really need a minimum spread of 25% to be viable.

The Property Insurance came from your Insurance Agent you're going to work with. You'll want an APPRAISAL up front, if you're paying ALL CASH because if you're borrowing money later to free up your Line of Credit, then you want to make sure your "in the market" on the properly.

Now about the Real Estate Commissions. The plan here is that your going to sell this home as a FSBO (For Sale By Owner), but time is of the essence so if a real estate agent brought you an offer, you've factored in a number to allow for that before you even bought the property. My 4% in this case is a low negotiated amount I have used many times. Commissions can range from around 3% to around 7%. Even as a FSBO, you can have an extra sign in the yard saying "Agents Welcome". What that means is that you're willing to pay them a Buyer Agent commission to sell your house that is not listed with a Realtor. You'll hear every excuse in the world how an agent HAS A BUYER FOR YOUR HOUSE, HOWEVER, Company Policy doesn't allow them to sell a FSBO and they MUST first LIST your house. BULL CRAP, to the power of 10 ! They can negotiate any commission they want. If they are restricted by their broker, then they don't have enough clout in the company to sell your property to begin with. If an Agent told ME that, my response would be "well, I'm offering the same 2.4% or 3% you'd get if it was listed with a real estate company and if you can't show and sell it for the same amount you'd get under those circumstances, I guess I'll just have to work with BROKERS than CAN make that decision".

Now . . . we've covered entering all the numbers and touched on some of the auto calculations from other numbers, but we haven't covered the second number, or last one which to decide . . . The Maximum Offering Price. Once you have entered everything but this, you then enter a number that is approximately 25% less than the amount you believe the property will sell for . . . the ReSale Amount. Since the Percent field is an auto-calculate, you can just keep entering numbers in the Maximum Offering Price cell until you reach at least a 25% spread. As soon as you've entered that number, look at the **Net Profit** number and the **Percentage Return** at the bottom. You need to have at least a 10% net profit return, and you want to make sure the dollar amount satisfies you as well. That's it. As I mentioned at the beginning of this section, if you want a free copy of my excel template, just send me an email and I'll email you a working copy to go from.

| | | | | | | |
|---|---|---|---|---|---|---|
| 1 | **Investment Analysis** | @ | 3/15/2014 | | | |
| 2 | 8022 Cloverhill, Little Rock AR  72205 | | | | | |
| 3 | Date of Projected Purchase: | 6/15/2008 | | 1,188 | sqft | |
| 4 | | | | | | |
| 5 | Re Sale Amount: | | $114,000 | $95.96 | | |
| 6 | MAXIMUM OFFERING PRICE | | $75,000 | $63.13 | $32.83 | |
| 7 | Discount of purchase to value | | $39,000 | 34% | | |
| 8 | | | | | | |
| 9 | Costs of Purchasing (closing costs): | | | | | |
| 10 | Plus: Property Insurance | 585 | | 4 months | | |
| 11 | Plus: Appraisal | 350 | | | | |
| 12 | Plus: Title Insurance at Purchase | 263 | 1,198 | | | |
| 13 | | | | | | |
| 14 | Additional Costs before Re-Sale: | | | { | UTILITIES BREAKDOWN | |
| 15 | Plus: Rehab Expense-Schedule (1) | 5,160 | | { | | |
| 16 | Plus: Utilities (Water, Gas, Electric) | 250 | 5,410 | →{ | | |
| 17 | | | | { | | |
| 18 | Costs of Re-Sale: | | | { | | |
| 19 | Prior Year RE Taxes-2007 | 0 | | | | |
| 20 | Current year RE Tax prorated-2008 | 491 | | | | |
| 21 | Termite Clearance | 250 | | { | | |
| 22 | Closing Fee (Doc Prep, Title Search & Close fee) | 410 | | { | | |
| 23 | Re-issue Title Insurance & Binder | 313 | | | | |
| 24 | Tax Report | 25 | | | 1/1/2008 | beginning tax year |
| 25 | State Revenue Stamps | 188 | | | 3/15/2014 | today |
| 26 | Record Power of Attorney | 0 | | | 8/15/2008 | closing |
| 27 | Buyer's Closing Costs | 0 | | | 6/15/2008 | purchase paid date |
| 28 | Real Estate Commission @ 4.0% (resell) | 4,560 | 6,237 | | 61 | days holding |
| 29 | | | | | | |
| 30 | Total Costs of Selling: | | 12,845 | | | |
| 31 | | | | | | |
| 32 | Financing Costs: | | | | | |
| 33 | Mortgage Interest at 6.0% | 830 | 830 | | 790 | Annual Tax |
| 34 | | | | | 227 | Days in year |
| 35 | NET PROFIT AFTER INTEREST & SALE: | | 25,326 | | | |
| 36 | Percentage Return | | 29% | | | |
| 37 | | | | | | |
| 38 | SUMMARY OF REHAB EXPENSE: | | | | | |
| 39 | Repair & New Seal Roof | 375.00 | (5-5gal buckets @ $45 bucket+$150) | | | |
| 40 | Paint Interior (paint material only) | 700.00 | (Kilz & Paint-10 galx2 x $35) | | | |
| 41 | Ceramic Tile Bathrooms & Kitchen | 500.00 | | | | |
| 42 | Replace kitchen counter & new sink | 385.00 | | | | |
| 43 | New Carpet | 1,000.00 | | | | |
| 44 | Repair Sheetrock & Replace Wood (leaks) | 200.00 | | | | |
| 45 | Miscellaneous | 2,000.00 | | | | |
| 46 | TOTAL (1) | 5,160.00 | | | | |
| | | | | | | |
| | Total Costs | $83,908 | | | | |
| | Total P&I Payment | 586.69 | | | | |
| | Tax Escrow payment | 65.83 | | | | |
| | Insurance payment | 48.75 | | | | |
| | TOTAL PAYMENT | 701.28 | | | | |
| | Plus Mgmt Fee | 70.00 | | | | |
| | Total | 771.28 | | | | |
| | Rent | 700.00 | | | | |
| | Net Rent | -71.28 | | | | |
| | | | | | | |
| | Total Costs | $83,908 | | | | |

# LESSON #15

## WHAT IS ASSET MANAGEMENT AND WHO ARE THESE PEOPLE?

Basically they are just middlemen. They're like computer geeks. Chances are they've never actually sold real estate personally. So their knowledge only goes so far in the realm of being "realistic" unless they work for an actual Real Estate Company. When a mortgage company (Bank) forecloses on a home and the bank is the highest bidder, the bank takes the deed of ownership in their name. From that point the bank generally hires a financial servicing company to dispose of the asset as they say. Sometimes the bank will hire this servicing company in advance of the actual foreclosure. Regardless, it's virtually impossible to track down who actually has the deciding power to sell a bank owned asset. These banks and lending institutions have an automatic system where they turn all their foreclosures over to an Asset Manager who actually performs the disposition function. They are the only one's that really know who has the say so at the bank. Many Asset Managers today are larger real estate companies that have an Asset Management Division that has several real estate salesman employees, that perform the same function as the HUD foreclosure properties agent. The Asset Manager works for the bank and is usually paid a flat fee for services performed plus a percentage fee for disposing (selling) the foreclosed home. The first item of business for the asset manager is to secure the home, obtain an appraisal, put the sign up and enter into the MLS system. So again, you can see those type of foreclosures don't produce any bargains in most cases.

Now there are situations where a small local bank might be foreclosing on a home and that bank has very few foreclosures and doesn't use the services of the larger asset management companies. If you have a relationship with a loan officer at that bank, you might be able to buy it for a decent discount to normal market values.

But keep in mind some basic common sense. What would happen if a bank foreclosed on an elderly woman with dementia, in a wheelchair on a $30,000 loan on a home worth $100,000? Do you honestly think the bank would sell to a buddy for $30,000 to recover their money? That would be very unethical and banks are held to a higher standard than that in the community, besides the fact there's no doubt some Federal Law that prevents that. The bank is required to make a reasonable effort to properly dispose of the asset and send any excess proceeds above the $30,000 to the foreclosed owner.

There are "Short Sales" that are another Buzz Term that I mentioned earlier, but those are also difficult and far and few between for good FLIP property. If you want a good summary of how Short Sales work, you can click on the link below to an article written in one of our newsletters, by one of our real estate agents that is also a mortgage broker that's done many short sale transactions. Written back in 2007, it's still a valid explanation today.

http://www.networkrealestatear.com/PageManager/Default.aspx/PageID=2067678&NF=1

# LESSON #16

## IN WHAT ORDER DO I PERFORM MY INVESTIGATIVE WORK?

 Ok, this is more or less a RECAP of what to do in the complicated process of buying a foreclosure or other distressed property. You don't want to be spending money for reports or information before your own due diligence justifies it. This assumes you've taken care of the beginning step of Talking To Your Banker and deciding where your Funds are going to come from. So use this as a guide in that process.

**(1) LOCATE:** Subscribe to a local foreclosure notice publication or get a copy from a real estate friend or read your local newspaper. Or use one of the other recommendations from the links I provided earlier.

**(2) PROPER AREA:** Stick to areas of town <u>you are familiar with</u> in your search for a foreclosed or special situation property or distressed property.

**(3) EAR TO GROUND:** Keep your ear to the ground for those special situation properties as described earlier and for those properties that get into a distressed situation. It might be a divorce or death or loss of a major job for the current owner.

**(4) CMA:** Once you've identified a potential property, obtain a CMA or Comparative Market Analysis on what that house might sell for in good condition from a Realtor that you're planning to work with.

**(5) TAX RECORD:** Obtain a copy of the Tax Record by going to your county tax office or calling them OR getting it on-line as most county offices have moved close into the 20th century. Most of the time the county will give you information on the telephone for free. And their fee for printing a copy of a document is pretty inexpensive. Do a Google search for their website as mentioned earlier.

**(6) MORTGAGE:** Now that you know the potential value and know what the county thinks the house is worth, you need to make a determination of the kind of debt that might be against that home. You can do this by checking with the county recording office on the mortgages that have been recorded. If the mortgage was recorded less than 2 years ago for almost the amount you think the house is worth . . . move on . . . there is no equity here to work with. If the mortgage is dated 5 to 8 years ago for a much smaller amount OR very old and there appears to be a 2nd or even 3rd mortgage AND the other mortgagees are different than the 1st mortgagee, then consider this a candidate.

**(7) D&D ANALYSIS:** Once it appears there is some equity in this potential investment, run your Down & Dirty analysis and determine the maximum you would be willing to pay for this house and then drive by and see if the home appears to be in good or poor physical condition. If the house looks like it's about to fall down . . . forget it, you'll have more headaches than you want. If you need to revise your repair estimate on your down and dirty, then do that at this point.

**(8) PHYSICAL CHECK:** while you're at the house, if the appearance looks good, knock on door and/or call the occupant and try to get into the home to walk through and tell them you deal in foreclosures and might be able to help them or at least give them some advice or direction to keep from losing their home. Generally the more disinterested you are in purchasing this house, the more good advice you give the owner on how to prevent a foreclosure. Right? If you can get in the door, you'll be miles ahead in your CSI investigation. Try to determine from the owner how much and how many mortgages they have and compare that to what you've found out so far. IF they only have one mortgage and there is a big spread between that mortgage and the estimated value, see if you can come to an agreement to buy the house to (1) save their credit and (2) provide them a small amount of cash to boot. Chances are, they will not go for your offer, but you've opened a line of communication that can be helpful later.

**(9) TITLE COMMITMENT:** If everything stills looks good to this point, buy a Title Search (Title Commitment) from your friendly title company that you're going to do all your business with. This will cost between $50 and $75 usually. It will show you all the liens, including IRS or mechanics liens, etc. to confirm what you've already discovered and maybe some things you weren't aware of.

**(10) BID-MAKE OFFER:** Ok, you've done your value analysis, you've made a drive by and you've entered all the numbers you know in your down and dirty analysis and you have a title search and know what the liens are. If everything still looks good, then you're ready to appear at the courthouse steps on the bid day if it's a courthouse step type property, and be prepared to bid your <u>maximum</u> bid. If very few competitor bidders are there that day, you could get lucky.

In my area there are about 15 homes a week on the Court House Step foreclosures. Of those, 3 to 5 will be canceled because the owner worked out an arrangement with the bank. Of the 10 or so left, only 1 or 2 will have an opening bid less than the maximum I'm willing to pay and of those 2 that are bid, a competitor will bid in excess of my maximum bid 9 out of 10 times. So this process is a lot of work for very very few hits. Now as a real estate agent, here is how quick and easy this information is for me to get. I have my legal notice foreclosure paper delivered every Tuesday, and I scan the summary by zip code to see what foreclosures there might be. Out of 20+ there may only be 2 or 3. I then pull the tax record online on my computer and print it out. Then I go into the MLS system and print a quick CMA based on that subdivision, which being in the business I am familiar with the neighborhoods. More than 90% of my foreclosures are handled by one foreclosure servicing company and their code ID case number contains the year in which the mortgage was initiated . . . so for example a case number 89-016422 means the mortgage was taken out in 1989. Now I know the value and county value and I then make a drive by. If all looks good, I go on-line in the county records and pull up all the liens and mortgages free and I save that to my file. If all still looks good I knock on the door of the house and see if I can get in . . . . usually can't. Now I enter the date of the mortgage, the amount of the original mortgage and interest rate into an excel spreadsheet to calculate what the exact mortgage balance should be now. Then I enter this data into my down and dirty excel format and it tells me the exact maximum I could bid on this property producing a spread of 25% between the cost and resell. Your profit won't be that much, but you have to have at least a 25% spread or it definitely won't be worth your time. Now I attempt to negotiate with the owner again and if not successful, I appear at the auction on Tuesday prepared to bid to a predetermined maximum amount. The opening bid from the bank should be about what I calculated and if a few regular bidders are sick that day, I might just get lucky and buy that house.

But, don't get too discouraged and not plan on bidding anymore because you <u>can</u> hit a home run every now and then. Those constant bidders that always show up at the auctions reach a point of saturation and purchase more than they need at times and might not show up to bid again for months at a time. And others that are fairly new to bidding wind up paying too much for a house and lose money and never show up again. I'd advise attending the auctions for at least a year before you decide you're not ever coming back.

Obviously the farther you live from the county courthouse, the more difficult time you're going to have. You'll be at a disadvantage in getting tax information and the time it takes to get to the auctions. The larger the city, the more foreclosures, but also that brings with it more competitor bidders. The advantage of the smaller cities and county foreclosures is less bidders.

On those properties you're looking at being sold by a Realtor that have an MLS listing, you can do all your work from that MLS information sheet and your CSI research. DON'T EVER be shy in making a Low Ball offer on a HUD or any other property, ESPECIALLY if it's been on the market for double the average sale time. At some point the seller is going to dump it and that day might be YOUR DAY. As I cited in one of my actual cases, I advised my client NOT to mess with lowering the price but he did, and he got it for even less, and it wasn't even a foreclosure!

# LESSON #17

## MORE ON SPECIAL SITUATIONS AND DISTRESSED PROPERTIES

As you can see from the information above, you can spend a lot of time and sometimes money, to get to the bidding table or making an offer, and very few times will you be successful in getting a Court House foreclosure. I have found that your time can be better spent and more productive in searching for those Special Situations and Distressed Properties. Always be mindful of what appears to be a vacant house and follow up on it . . . everyone else is too busy to notice. Talk about your buying venture to everyone you meet . . . they may refer you to somebody.

Use the Shotgun Approach. Take at shot at Anything! Spend some time checking on a few obituaries in the paper or divorce filings. You might find a situation where an elderly person has passed away and the nearest relative lives out of state and they simply do not want to fool with disposing of the home, or a divorce situation that results in a spouse that can't really afford to keep making payments for a long period of time on their own. I've seen many a foreclosure that started out as a divorce . . . the house was deeded to a spouse and then 12 months later a foreclosure action came up. They are having a difficult time changing their standard of living.

Talk to a few bank real estate loan officers and see if they can provide you some good leads and talk to a few real estate agents that are in the know. Even though their in the business, rarely do they buy what they sell every day. You can purchase blank stock Business Card paper from Office Depot and make yourself a Business Card like "Smith's Home Purchasing", etc. to pass out. I usually only print 10 cards at a time so I can keep changing it up a bit with information on the back of the card.

NOTE: There are also GOOD deals that come from just "keeping your ear to the ground" so to speak. In other words, tell all your neighbors and friends that you buy distressed property to fix up . . . post it on your FaceBook page . . . get the word out however you can. I have found several houses where the owner was very old . . . either moved into a nursing home and selling through an agent, or had passed away and heirs were in another state and were selling the house through an agent and they were not interested in making "Top Market Value" . . . they just wanted what's called "FREE FAST CASH", like a lottery ticket winner. In those cases, the house might be worth $100,000 and the agent tells them that but they want to sell in less then 30 days and so he lists it for $80,000 and you offer $60,000 and they take it. That does happen as well. That's why it helps to RESEARCH a potential house . . . research the asking price, potential price, repairs needed, who the owner is, the "situation" like a death, estate, divorce, etc. Why not set up a FREE Company FaceBook page? Jim's Home Purchasing & Rehab/FLIP. Put the page to PRIVATE, only for viewing by those in your Friend list so you don't get someone in Kokomo, Indiana wanting to selling you a $2,000 shack.

Since my original writing of this book and eBook, I have ended my personal involvement in "partnering" up with my investor clients considering it a conflict of interest in dealing with the various Investors I work with, but rather just find my Investors the deals and take my commission if they purchase and then sell it for them when needed, and let my Investor/Buyer retain all the profits. I treat my regular Occupant Home Buyers the same way. If they want a Great Bargain house and they're not in a hurry, we go after one of these special type deals.

Another type house to really take serious is the VACANT home. It could be a real Sleeper. Sometimes neighbors get so used to living next door to a vacant home they just forget all about it. In my searching for bargain deals several years ago, I noticed a home that "sort of" looked like it might be vacant, even though the grass was cut. It was also within a half block of a lake. It was a 1 story, all brick home. I drove by the house often and decided to look in the windows after I saw a bunch of mail falling out of the street mailbox. Looking in the windows, it was obvious it was vacant and had been for quite a while. I pulled up the tax records and other information and it appeared to be owned by an attorney after doing my extensive (CSI) Comprehensive Search Investigation. Then I proceeded to find the attorney. After 2 months of research, I discovered (1) the attorney died 7 years ago (2) he was in a hospital and fell in love with his nurse and married her with a prenuptial agreement (3) there was NO debt or mortgage on the house (4) the attorney had 2 male grown children, both rumored to be fairly irresponsible and living out of state (5) the neighbor was cutting the grass (6) the "wife" just up and left for Dallas since she had no legal interest in the house (7) the attorney charged with "probating the will" had never done so and STILL was showing it as an "open case". (8) in Arkansas, if you do not probate a will within 5 years, it's void and null as though no will existed. (9) This means you have to probate the estate intestate (absent a will).

I attempted to meet with this less than adept attorney that never probated the will thinking he would be motivated to making some good money by "handling this estate" and finding the heirs and disposing of the real property and make a lot of money, but I couldn't even get him tied down long enough to discuss it in person. I "somehow" got into the house and took pictures, did my market analysis and figured I could get one of my investors to just make a CASH offer to the attorney for $50,000 for a potential $160,000 FLIP house and get him off dead center. I think I located one of the sons in Florida and another in a northern state but before I could contact them to work a deal direct . . . . all of a sudden, out of the clear blue after this house sat there for 7 years vacant, one of the son's just "appeared"... takes physical possession of the house, fires the attorney... appoints himself as executor of the estate, lives in the house, fixes it up and STOLE my deal !! Lesson learned here is when you find out a lot of good information on a good potential FLIP... keep the information close to the vest and don't say too much to too many outsiders. The attorney no doubt shot his mouth off, cutting me out of the deal and the irresponsible son cut HIM out of the deal as well.

On another good lead, I used to sell a lot of property in an area known as Lake Norrell in Alexander, Arkansas. It's an area with a 280 acre lake approximately 90 feet deep with 230 homes on 330 acres. Very secluded and very popular. Generally there are no more than 2 or 3 sales max a year. After building a very comprehensive database of information on all the property, I found several deals. One of the best was 2 nice cabins with about 1,000 square feet on the water that had been vacant for at least 5 years. I traced the possible owner to a woman that supposedly had gone bonkers years ago and moved to Lonoke, AR. The property was Delinquent in Real Estate Tax, and turned out to be a TAX DEED SALE by the State Land Commissioner. Another area of potential deals but not near as lucrative or easy to do as Foreclosures. In Arkansas, you have to stop making tax payments for 3 years before the county turns the deed over to the State. Then the state keeps the deed for another 2 years before they set up a Tax Deed Sale in the 5th or 6th year. I was all set to buy these two parcels in about 30 days when all of a sudden her brother, a local "politician" must have got wind and paid the tax current. This is what is called "redeeming" the property. I'd been following this property for over a year. Problem with Tax Deeds though is that after you successfully buy the property, the original owner still has another 12 Months to "redeem" the deed, meaning that if during the next 12 months they decided to take their property back, all they had to pay me was the amount I paid. So IF you made any improvements on a property like this... you LOSE all your improvement investment!

Without going into all the detail, there is another parcel of land on Lake Norrell I've been watching that has about 600 foot frontage on the lake and with a run down mobile home on it. It's actually 5 plotted lots all owned by one individual as one parcel. The whole property could be purchased for around $70,000 and someone could build 5 small cabins and make an excellent return. Lot's of complications in the deal with sewer lines, grading a new road on a 45 degree mountain, but for the right investor, I have a deal for him.

# LESSON #18

## ACTION SUMMARY

Ok . . . here are the STEPS TO TAKE. <u>Provided</u> you know where your cash funds are coming from to make a foreclosure or distressed home purchase, and you have chosen a Real Estate Agent, a Banker or Money Partner, a Title Company and an Insurance Agent, and a source for reading about the foreclosures coming up, here is a quick summary of the steps to take.

_____ (1) Identify the potential foreclosure or distressed property

_____ (2) Use your CMA Comparative Market Analysis to determine the CURRENT "As Is" MARKET VALUE

_____ (3) Use the CMA to determine the AFTER rehab resale value

_____ (4) Obtain a copy of the Tax Record

_____ (5) Obtain a copy of the Mortgage

_____ (6) Calculate the approximate current Mortgage Balance

_____ (7) Run your Down & Dirty Analysis for Rate of Return

_____ (8) Drive by the house for a Physical Inspection and determine if you can make contact with the current owner

_____ (9) Obtain a Title Search to determine all mortgages and liens

_____ (10) Show up at the courthouse steps and make your maximum bid

_____ (11) OR Negotiate with your Agent on a price to offer HUD or whomever the seller is

_____ (12) Pay for the property if you're the successful bidder/buyer

_____ (13) Take Physical Possession of the house

_____ (14) Make your repairs per your budget & plan

_____ (15) Place the house on the market for sale

_____ (16) Attend the closing, deposit your fat check in the bank and take your spouse out to a Celebration Dinner.

# LESSON #19

**REMEMBER . . .**

## KNOWLEDGE IS POWER . . .

## POWER PROPERTY APPLIED CAN BE WEALTH !

*I could teach a Class with just this information, pump you up, convince you that YOU CAN do this and charge you $2,500. I could tell you how I'm going to HOLD YOUR HAND, be there for you EVERY STEP OF THE WAY, be your MONEY PARTNER, etc. The odds are that for every 1,000 people I teach, I would have 1% or 10 people that would be successful because they have the right collection of motivation, resources and skill and I can then Advertise their Success Stories as "**see . . . I told you that ordinary people can do this**", but 990 people failed and flushed $2,500 down the toilet and I made more money telling you "How" to do it than I would have made in actually Doing it. All because it IS possible to do all these things but FINDING the deals is the secret. Don't be fooled.*

David W. Bolick, Licensed Real Estate Broker, 43+ years.
dbonweb@aol.com
Last revision dated 03/15/2014

www.ingramcontent.com/pod-product-compliance
Lightning Source LLC
Chambersburg PA
CBHW050746180526
45159CB00003B/1371